MARATHON
DAD

MARATHON

DAD

SETTING A PACE THAT WORKS FOR WORKING FATHERS

JOHN EVANS

AVON BOOKS  NEW YORK

AVON BOOKS, INC.
1350 Avenue of the Americas
New York, New York 10019

Copyright © 1998 by John A. Evans
Cover photograph by Scott Barrow
Inside back cover author photo by Elena Anastas-Evans
Interior design by Rhea Braunstein
Published by arrangement with the author
ISBN: 0-380-79321-0
www.avonbooks.com

Library of Congress Cataloging in Publication Data:

Evans, John, 1952–
Marathon dad : setting a pace that works for working fathers / John Evans.
p.   cm.
1. Fathers—United States—Psychology. 2. Fathers—Employment—United States.
3. Work and family—United States—Psychological aspects. I. Title.
HQ756.E92   1998   98-4033
306.874'2—dc21   CIP

First Avon Books Trade Paperback Printing: September 1999
First Avon Books Hardcover Printing: October 1998

AVON TRADEMARK REG. U.S. PAT. OFF. AND IN OTHER COUNTRIES, MARCA REGISTRADA, HECHO EN U.S.A.

Printed in the U.S.A.

OPM 10 9 8 7 6 5 4 3 2 1

To my Dad, who, after seventy-six trips around the Sun, continues to be my model for Teacher, Nurturer, Protector, and Provider.

▼   ▼   ▼   ▼

Acknowledgments

▼ ▼ ▼ ▼

There are many people to whom I am indebted for this book.

I am most grateful to Dan Klein for his guidance, expertise, and patience throughout this project. Our office sessions were packed with great ideas. His sense of organization and his creativity are fabulous gifts.

My sincere appreciation to Howard Morhaim for his faith in my work, and to the Morhaim Literary Agency for their hard work on behalf of *Marathon Dad*. I cannot express my thanks fully enough to Lou Aronica and the staff at Avon Books for having the vision and wisdom to publish this book.

Thanks to Freke Vuijst for her reading and feedback on *Marathon Dad*.

I am deeply indebted to Kevin Doscher, PsyD, for sharing his intriguing thesis on fathering roles. Dr. Doscher's application of a multigenerational context and social construct thinking gave me a substantial foothold for the development of this book. His work is creative and significant.

I am grateful to the families who have allowed me to use their stories as case examples in this work. Their hard work and sharing is a key to the success of the book.

Sincere thanks to Ellen Bankert and the Center for Work and Family in Boston, Massachusetts, for being so hospitable, and for providing me with valuable material. Also, appreciation to Beverly

Carothers of the Polaroid Corporation for sharing policy ideas and pointing me in the direction of the New England Work and Family Association.

My warmest thanks and love to my partner in the real life marathon of being parents, Elena Anastas-Evans. She gives real meaning to the term "partner" as she shares the work, joys, laughter and tears of our family life. To my young lions, Ian, Colin, and Owen, I give my thanks for teaching me over and over again what it is like to learn, grow, challenge, and change. You are my great pride and loving joy.

My love to Lillian and Paul Evans for getting me far enough and then letting go. Thanks also to my sisters and brothers, as well as "The Outlaws": Paul Evans, Julia Evans, Rich Bourgelas, Chris and Mary Dansereaux, Gerald and Linda Evans, Chip and Kathy Chapin, Ricky and Patty Landry, Paul and Anne Kippetz. You've regularly shown me the way.

A very special thanks to Mary Anastas for her strength and love, and Ken Frisbee (The SRU-5000) for his tools, know-how, and smiles. I owe a debt of gratitude for the companionship and support of John and Harriet Anastas, Gary and Ceres Zabel, and Mike and Eoana Sturges, and my wonderful nieces and nephews (CCIB Forever).

I appreciate the support of my colleagues at the South County Psychiatric and Psychotherapy Center in Great Barrington, Massachusetts, particularly Dennis Marcus, MD, and Jeff Forget, MA. I am also thankful for the ongoing support of Trinity College of Vermont's Program in Community Mental Health, in particular Paul Carling, PhD., Laurie Curtis, MSW, Annamarie Ciofarri, MSW, and Susan Biss, MSW. Also, my gratitude goes to fellow coaches Mike Powell, Sean Flynn, and Bill Eigen, for consistently letting me duck out the warmups for that extra fifteen minutes. I couldn't have finished this project without the support of all of you.

The help, support, love and dialogue of friends has been invaluable in my work. Thanks to Ed, Kathy, Mike, Miriam, Jim, Sally, Mark, Arti, Renzo, Barbara, Eugene, Maureen, Sheila, and Fran. Additional thanks to Mike Silsby and Alex Sabo for their encouragement and sense of humor, both in the office and on the chair lift. Also, my genuine gratitude to Ray Brien for his mentorship and for knowing when to open the corral gate and push me through it.

Finally, I want to acknowledge my connection to the Berkshires— its lakes, frozen or melted; its hills and woods lush with pine and mountain laurel, green year round. The chance to retreat and reflect here is something unique and incredibly precious to me.

Contents

▼ ▼ ▼ ▼

PART II: PRACTICES
Setting a Pace That Works with Honest Priorities, Effective Time Managment, and Clear Communications

PART III: POLITICS
Taking the Lead to a Marathon-Dad-Friendly Work Culture

MARATHON
DAD

Introduction

▼ ▼ ▼ ▼

I recognize him by his gait the moment he enters my office for the first time: brisk, determined, yet with more than a hint of frenzy. There are bags under his eyes. Before he utters a word, he shoots a quick glance at his watch. He seems both highly competent and utterly fragmented, a man whose various parts don't quite fit together comfortably. And finally, I spot the telltale sign: peeping over the top of the breast pocket of his blazer is a blunt nub of tan plastic—a pacifier!

It's another Marathon Dad—another breathless man trying to juggle the demands of a full-time career and hands-on, involved parenting in a two-working-parent home.

As an increasing number of overtired, guilty, and conflicted Marathon Dads began showing up in my therapy practice these past few years, I realized that these men's problems and frustrations differed significantly from those of their female counterparts, Super Moms. At work, Marathon Dads receive even less support for their responsibilities as an equal-time parent. Not only is time off from work for parenting duties more grudgingly granted—if it is granted at all—but macho peer pressure is always there with a ready sardonic smile and a remark such as, "A woman's work is never done, eh, pal?" On top of this, men bear the responsibility of being a bread-winner more heavily than most women do, whether in financial fact or just in their minds. Similarly, the drive to succeed in a career and the corollary fear of failing at it appear to take up much more troubling emotional space in men's lives than in most women's.

Meanwhile, back on the home front, men feel less naturally gifted at parenting than women do, a feeling that is often subtly reinforced by wives who persist in protecting their traditional sphere of expertise, even if they are themselves working mothers who believe in equally shared parental roles. Aggravating this insecurity about our male parenting instincts and know-how is the fact that most of us did not have role models in our own fathers for how an involved, hands-on working father should conduct himself. Put together, these pressures and stereotypes set the Marathon Dad on a breakneck course fraught with hurdles and quicksand.

But this is not a plea for pity for Dad. I am not crying to the working mothers of the world, "Hey, we've got problems too!" On the contrary, the central motif of my practice with working fathers—and the central theme of this book—is that the problems of being a Marathon Dad and of being a Super Mom are *shared* problems. The readjustment of roles, the guilt over not giving enough to either work or family, the confusions of transitioning from the world of work to the world of family and back again, the relentless exhaustion and all the debilities that come along with that exhaustion—these are problems that neither Dad nor Mom can resolve alone or in a vacuum.

I have come to think of good shared-parenting and home-choring as a relay race, a two-person team going the distance, meeting each other halfway in full stride and, with one fluid, well-practiced motion, passing the baton without losing a step.

Essential to success is knowing your own stride and pace, and trusting your partner's ability to do the same *in her own style*.

That is the key right there: acknowledging the differences in style that make Mom a *mom* and Dad a *dad*. Ignoring these differences or denying them in the name of some kind of gender ideology turns out to be the underlying cause of many of the individual frustrations and marriage tensions for both Marathon Dad and Super Mom. There is a raft of research that shows just how thoroughgoing these differences in parenting styles are and how marvelously complementary they can be when recognized and appropriately exploited. Happily, *both* parenting styles count in developing a healthy, balanced, well-adjusted child. Getting to know what is unique about being a father (as compared to that Jekyll-and-Hyde ordeal of trying to be both a father and a mother) is one of the first orders of business in this book.

But lest any of you fellow fathers in two-working-parent families think that saying, "Dad is a dad and can only be a dad," will let you off the hook when it comes to, say, changing diapers or driving Jennifer to ballet class, I hate to disappoint you, but it just ain't so. The programs and guidance set forth in *Marathon Dad* will definitely make your lives *easier* and *infinitely more satisfying*, but there is still a load of work to be done and only two of you to do it.

There is, of course, a growing number of Marathon Dads who divide parenting in shared-custody families, and they have a distinct set of problems and frustrations, but virtually all the principles of joint parenting that I explore in this book apply as much to shared-custody dads as to married Marathon Dads.

For me, a veteran Marathon Dad with three young sons and a wife who works full-time, the worst pitfall any of us can fall into is *failing to fully enjoy both of our roles*—worker *and* parent. When two-career families became the norm and we first realized that we were going to have to shoulder some of the responsibilities of parenting as well as holding down a job, many of us reacted with resentment. "This isn't the deal I signed up for!" we protested. But gradually, a great many of us discovered that genuine hands-on parenting could be a source of incredible pleasure. And, what's more, that at its best it could be a wonderful antidote to the aggressiveness and cheerlessness of the daily grind. In fact, many of us came to the realization that being a truly involved parent was a privilege that previous generations of dads had been denied.

Marathon Dad is both a practical and a psychological guide to solving the problems inherent to combining career and fatherhood. But beyond simply resolving these problems is a much grander goal: *taking our place as leaders of a fundamental shift in the history of men.*

1

But First, a Word from
Our Reality Checker

▼ ▼ ▼ ▼

Are You Really Sure You Want to Go Down This Road?

When it comes to our express desire to be first-rate, hands-on, fully committed fathers, we often gaze at the prospect through heavily tinted glasses. We tend to envision our increased commitment to fathering as taking place on the Little League field watching Junior steal second base, not in the vestibule of the dentist's office waiting for Junior to have his molars yanked. We imagine being a New Dad who helps the kids with homework and engages them in heart-to-heart chats about Love and Life, not a New Dad who changes diapers and packs school lunches.

The truth is that a fully committed father is *all* of the above—he's there at Little League *and* in the dentist's waiting room; he's supervising homework *and* he's packing lunch. To get around confronting this home truth, we dads have been known to come up with some pretty tricky alibis and delusions; many of us talk the talk of Committed Fatherhood without really wanting to walk the walk. We may proudly go public with our belief in parenting equality, but we somehow manage to plead extenuating circumstances *every* time our wives remind us that it is our turn to drive Jennifer to her ballet lesson.

I'm afraid that won't cut it here. Not because I have some doctrinaire idea of exactly what a New Dad is supposed to do or be—believe me, I have a deep-seated aversion to political correctness, especially around issues of fatherhood. No, the reason that kind of New Dad Doublethink won't cut it here is because the first step to reconciling Fully Committed Fatherhood with a Fully Committed Career is a genuine consciousness of who we are, what we want, and what we are capable of doing. Anything less than that kind of personal honesty will only lead to more confusion—and confusion is a major enemy when it comes to balancing fatherhood with career.

Seven Good Reasons for Dropping Out of the Marathon

So before we make any pledges to ourselves or to anyone else, let's take a brutally honest look at the real life of Day-to-Day Dad:

1. A lot of what he does is drudge work and grunge work. We're talking diaper detail, endless chauffeuring, and a healthy dose of sick-bed baby-sitting here—*although, as we will see, some of the drudge and grunge can be "outsourced" to newly developing family service industries without short-changing our kids, emotionally or otherwise.*

2. The hours are long. It turns out that every working parent's favorite alibi—"A few hours of Quality Time with my kids is more valuable than several hours of low-quality time"— is little more than a self-serving myth. In order to be a genuinely felt presence in our children's lives, we simply have to put in long hours with them, high quality or low. *Yet, as we will see,* *there are ways to make many of those hours highly productive for other areas of our lives, including our jobs.*

3. A lot of the work is boring. Any man who has watched *Mr. Rogers* with his toddler knows what I'm talking about here, as does any man who has helped his fourth grader memorize the state capitals. *Still, as we will demonstrate, one man's boredom can be another man's stress-reduction exercise.*

4. The pay stinks. If you have any doubts about this, ask any housewife—your mother, for example. *Yet isn't there something liberating about passing some time that does not have a monetary value attached to it?*

5. There are no guaranteed product results. The fact that you are a first-rate, hands-on, fully committed father does not ensure that your child will get into Harvard or even that he will stay out of trouble. You improve the odds, to be sure, but sorry, no guarantees. *On the other hand, you drastically improve the odds that your child will be happy, secure, and self-confident . . . which some people believe is even more valuable than a Harvard education.*

6. Kids can be rats. What I am talking about here is spending two hours patiently helping your son with his algebra homework and then having him thank you by saying, "Geez, that was a drag. I'm glad you're not my *real* math teacher." Actually, this is just a mild example of the rat problem. *And yet, after all is said and done, the boy is learning from you and he is your very own rat.*

7. The job of parenting is so aggravating that even mothers would rather be at work than at home. This last point was revealed only recently in a study that showed that most working women found more interest, emotional support, and relative calm in the workplace than at home. It came as a terrible disillusionment to many of us who still secretly believed that when push came to shove, the best deal of all was being a housewife. Now we're stuck with the idea that not even women genuinely like the work of parenting, so how could we possibly like it ourselves? *Unless, of course, we men*

*are just coming in touch with something that many women
are starting to lose touch with . . .*

So What's in It for Me?

Most of us know the answer to this one, otherwise we wouldn't
be reading a book called *Marathon Dad*. But after those seven
chilling reasons for dropping out of the race, it is probably a
good idea to refresh our memories about why we actually do
want to stay in it. So here are

Seven Overwhelmingly Good Reasons for Staying in the Marathon

1. We love our kids and want what is best for them.
There, I said it. The question is, of course, what exactly *is*
best for them? (See below.)

**2. We know in our heart of hearts that our children
get something valuable from fathers that no one else can
give them, not even their mothers.** We're talking about
role modeling, emotional and cognitive balancing, and a certain sense of security for everyone, among many other things.
(I told you I wasn't politically correct.)

**3. We honestly believe that there is more to handing
down family tradition than giving our children our name
and our money.** That means passing along our personal values, skills, ways of seeing things, and ways of doing things.
And we know that those things will never get handed down
if our children spend little time with us as compared to the
time they spend with their teachers, friends, and television
role models.

**4. We know that when our children have grown up
and gone away, we'll regret every hour we could have
spent with them but did not.** Most of us are familiar with this
particular nightmare: that we wake up one morning to discover
that it is too late to fulfill our good intentions for fatherhood—

too late because the children have grown up, or worse, because the children are already alienated from us. Fulfilling those good intentions now is a preemptive strike on future regrets.

5. We realize that our kids can be the source of many of our absolutely happiest moments. There are all kinds of such moments, but the ones I happen to value the most are when one of my children puts me in contact with my long-suppressed *playful* self—that guy who can stand on his head, giggle, or lie on his back in a field and play "cloud shapes" as if he were still ten years old and not a full-grown man loaded with full-grown man responsibilities.

6. We realize that genuine fathering nourishes some of the best but oft-neglected parts of our character. Egocentrism, narcissism, and competitiveness usually get plenty of nourishment at work. What a marvelous antidote it is to come home to children who need our attention and patience—who can pull us out of our egos for at least part of the day. And speaking of antidotes, there is a mysterious process that goes on when we become the father to our children that we wish our own father had been to us—it is known as "refathering ourselves" and it can make us a hell of a lot more content and mentally healthy as grown men.

7. We honestly believe in fair play and at rock bottom we know that it is not fair to let our working wives do the lion's share of the work at home and with the children. I saved this little gem of moral rectitude for last because it is not one of my favorite reasons for being a fully committed father. It lacks a certain joie de vivre, if you follow my meaning. Nonetheless, it is obviously a good and just reason for doing our fair share of parenting.

Thus ends the word from our Reality Checker. We all know what we really want to do: we can dither about it or we can get on with it. My job is to demonstrate to you *how* we can get on with being both a First-Rate Father and a First-Rate Worker as consciously, efficiently, and happily as possible.

2

A Tale of Two Masters

▼ ▼ ▼ ▼

The problems facing Marathon Dad are as fundamental as
they get. They come down to questions like, "How can I be
in two places at one time?" and "How can I do my best at
two conflicting tasks?" and "How can I love two things
equally?" They are the age-old problems of serving two demanding masters—or pleasing two exacting mistresses. Marathon Dad is perpetually confronting choices between Work
and Home, Career and Fatherhood, and the consequences of
choosing one over the other pile guilt upon panic upon
exhaustion.

How can a man be both a First-Rate, Fully Committed
Father and a First-Rate, Fully Committed Professional? To
find the answer to that question, we need to start by examining
the basic characteristics of each.

The Ten Characteristics of a First-Rate, Fully Committed Father

1. **He puts Fatherhood on a par with—or ahead of—
   every other endeavor in his life.**
2. **He never uses work obligations as an excuse for**

doing less than his share of work at home or for being less than a fully committed father.

3. He shares equally with his wife the workload of being a parent.

4. He embraces every aspect of fathering, from Nurturer to Disciplinarian to Teacher to Drudge Worker.

5. He is never afraid to stand up for the idea of Fatherhood that he believes in—both at work *and* with his wife.

6. He loves his children and is never afraid to show it.

7. He never apologizes to his employer or colleagues for his loyalty to his family.

8. He is mindful of planning his family duties.

9. He acknowledges his place in the Historical Legacy of Fatherhood.

10. He champions good Fatherhood with his fellow fathers.

The Ten Characteristics of a First-rate, Fully Committed Professional

1. He puts Career on a par with—or ahead of—every other endeavor in his life.

2. He never uses fatherhood obligations as an excuse for doing less than a first-rate job and he never does less than his share at work because of family obligations.

3. He meets all professional expectations and deadlines.

4. He does whatever it takes to get his job done well, from taking on leadership to doing drab-but-necessary tasks.

5. He is never afraid to take a stand on a professional idea that he believes in.

6. He loves his job and is never afraid to show it.
7. He never apologizes to his family for his loyalty to his job.
8. He recognizes the cardinal importance of time management as a professional; he is well organized and goal-directed.
9. He acknowledges his place in the Historical Legacy of a Professional Worker.
10. He champions Professionalism with his fellow workers.

Irreconcilable Differences?

These two lists stand like enemies screaming at one another across a chasm. Each demands to be taken seriously. Each demands to be honored. And each demands to come first. Point by point, they appear to be utterly irreconcilable. Nevertheless, not only *can* they be reconciled, but they can be reconciled in ways that make us both better fathers *and* better professionals.

The reconciliation of each of these seemingly opposing characteristics is the basic agenda of this book: Each chapter that follows develops ideas and techniques that bridge the gap between them. In general, these reconciliations happen in three places: **Our Heads**, where the road to reconciliation is found in breaking down stereotypes and shifting mind-sets; **Our Practices**, where new adaptive techniques of time management, communication, and negotiation make life at both work and home more effective and more satisfying; and **Our Politics**, where we can act as agents of change in the culture of the workplace and in the culture of the family.

Okay, let's get back to those two lists and lay the groundwork for how we can reconcile being a First-Rate, Fully Committed Father with being a First-Rate, Fully Committed Professional. Following are the basic reconciliations; the details of how to make these reconciliations happen is the substance of the rest of this book.

1. **He puts Fatherhood on a par with—or ahead of—every other endeavor in his life / He puts Career on a par with—or ahead of—every other endeavor in his life.**

Our Heads: A man who constantly feels divided allegiances and dithers between them is a man who will always feel beset by guilt and confusion. But *two* allegiances do not have to mean *divided* allegiances. If you know your own priorities and trust your judgment to pick them out as alternatives present themselves, you will not feel constantly torn between two masters. You simply know that your child comes first in certain situations and that your business comes first in others: You know that when, by your standards, your child *really* needs you and no one else, you will be there and nothing will stand in your way. The key to getting there is embracing the fact that *you* are ultimately the only person in charge of setting your own priorities—not your wife, not your boss, and not your kids.

Our Practices: We think through and establish a checklist of priorities—maxims for choices that we can feel comfortable with and confident in. An easy example of a priority: *family medical emergencies always take precedence over any demand at work.* A tougher example: *a high fever rarely counts as a medical emergency.* Once we establish clear priorities, we will behave consistently.

We communicate our priorities loud and clear to everyone involved both at home and at work so that there are seldom any surprises on either front. Our children are secure in the knowledge that when they *really* need us, we will be there for them; our boss and fellow workers are secure in the knowledge that when they *really* need us, we will be there for them.

Finally, we are always open to revising our priorities based on input from others at work and at home.

Our Politics: A major fallout of the above communication will be to set new collective standards of what are legitimate demands of family and work as compared to what are merely artifacts from outdated gender politics and power politics. We set an example that helps everyone sort out which policies contribute to productivity and which simply continue to contribute to make-work and arbitrary tests of loyalty. Our personal example says: *I can be loyal to my job without being a slave to it; and I can be loyal to my family without indulging its every desire.*

2. **He never uses work obligations as an excuse for doing less than his share of work at home or for being less than a fully committed father / He never uses fatherhood obligations as an excuse for doing less than a first-rate job and he never does less than his share at work because of family obligations.**

Our Heads: The common denominator here is excuse-making, a veritable industry for many of us. Our mothers were right about this one: if we are looking for an excuse for not doing something, we'll find one—and it will even sound pretty good. The reason we make excuses is because they work (in the short term) and because we can get away with them. For many men, excuses are a cultural habit on the home front: we heard our fathers make them all the time.

But making excuses turns out to be *extremely* counterproductive for Marathon Dads. Excuse-making is the psychological ally of a divided-loyalties mind-set; as long as we are busy making excuses for doing A rather than B, we never have to get around to *prioritizing A and B*. The end result is that we spend more time and energy making excuses than we would if we resolved our priorities and put an end to our need for excuses. We finally realize that if our task has become that of excusing ourselves from tasks, we have lost focus on what we really want to get done.

Our Practices: Because we have established and communicated our priorities, we find ourselves making fewer and fewer excuses at home and at work. We don't have to anymore, because everyone knows what to expect of us. As a result, we are far better focused and get more done in both places.

Our Politics: Giving up excuse-making represents a bigger cultural shift than most of us would imagine. In the old family culture when women did not go to work, men were pretty much expected to use their jobs as an excuse for not pitching in at home. That doesn't cut it now; still, it is taking a long time for family culture to adjust to that fact, and it is the responsibility of Marathon Dad to help that adjustment along.

On the other hand, some working mothers have allowed excuse-making to seep into the new workplace culture—excuses on the order of "I didn't do a good job because I was too busy being a good mommy." Permitting excuse-making at work is a cultural shift that ultimately is counterproductive for both working mothers and working fathers; the political responsibility of Marathon Dad here is to resist such a cultural shift.

3. He shares equally with his wife the workload of being a parent / He meets all professional expectations and deadlines.

Our Heads: We start by admitting to ourselves once and for all that times have changed, women are staying in the workforce, so we have to get past the old "I already gave at the office" mind-set. But by the same token, we recognize that one reason we resist equally sharing the workload at home is because we confuse *equal tasks* with *identical tasks*; we confuse doing home tasks in a *characteristically male way* with doing them in a *neutered parental way*, a way that may not come easily or naturally to us. (No, I am not setting up some macho excuse for getting out of work here, just introducing a critical distinction that runs throughout this book: namely, that *a dad is not a mom*.) Getting beyond these confusions requires resisting a load of guilt, some of it perpetuated by confused wives.

Similarly, as professionals who meet all on-the-job expectations and deadlines, we value our own personal style of doing our job; we realize that we do not have to conform to some anonymous model of a good worker as long as we get the job done. We are confident and secure enough to take advantage of changes in the workplace that have been brought about by working mothers (say flex time) without being cowed by male stereotypes (like, "Only a wimp would take flex time").

Our Practices: At home, we negotiate with our wives a way of doing our fair share of the second shift, and then we do our fair share without making excuses. *But we explicitly reserve the right to do our share in our own way, preserving our own fathering aptitudes and styles*. For example, we may declare that we will share diaper-changing duties, but we also declare that *we* decide when and how we will do it—mothers cannot insist on being the "experts" who make those decisions for us.

At work, we learn from pioneering working mothers which of the new family/work programs actually work and which do not. As long as we are able to continue doing a first-rate job while using these programs, we are not afraid to use them.

Our Politics: We participate in a major shift here—from the lingering pre-women-at-work division of labor (women take care of all home duties) to a division of home tasks determined by fairness. We begin negotiating our tasks with our wives by immediately acknowledging that we want to reach parity; but we also insist that they respect our personal and characteristic gender differences in doing our share. We define ourselves in the workplace as someone committed to doing an A-one job *and* being an equal-share parent.

Both of these political positions involve revised definitions of being a man; at home, we define being a father as categorically different from being a mother; at work, we define being a male worker with parenting responsibilities as categorically *similar to* being a female worker with parenting responsibilities—and we do not apologize for that similarity.

4. **He embraces every aspect of fathering, from Nurturer to Disciplinarian to Teacher to Drudge Worker / He does whatever it takes to get his job done well, from taking on leadership to doing drab-but-necessary tasks.**

Our Heads: We do not let stereotypes of fatherhood foisted on us by women, other men, our parents, and popular culture prevent us from taking on this role in all of its varieties and complexities. We acknowledge that being a father is *not* one thing.

When it comes to the ever-present problem of doing the drudge work of parenting, we find that reconciliation comes by applying a standard from our work lives to our home lives: at time or another, most of us have done some drudge work in order to bring in needed income and most of us are proud of having done so; but at home, many of us have drawn the line at doing crap work (literally, as in changing a diaper) because we are *too proud* to do it, because we persist in calling it "women's work." A fond farewell to that stereotype.

We are now ready to acknowledge the fact that there is the same honor in doing drudge work at home as there is in doing it to earn money. Similarly, we are also ready to acknowledge that there is the same honor in being a "team player" at home as there is in being a "team player" at work.

Our Practices: We do the jobs we say we will do at both work and home.

Our Politics: Again, we are point men in the major cultural shift from fathers who do not do their fair share to fathers who do.

5. He is never afraid to stand up for the idea of Fatherhood that he believes in—both at work *and* with his wife / He is never afraid to take a stand on a professional idea that he believes in.

Our Heads: The common denominators here are *confidence* and *independence of thought.* We need them both to resist the stereotypes of fatherhood and maleness that everyone and his mother (literally) seem to want to foist on us. As confident and independent Marathon Dads, we will not let anyone else define us or our roles, not a wife who insists on being the "expert" at home, not a male peer who insists that only wimps take paternity leave.

Our Practices: We go public with our personal convictions at both home and work. (Otherwise, we haven't really taken a stand anywhere but in our heads.) We absorb the consequences of our stands, including enduring some marital conflict and some peer disapproval.

Our Politics: Our convictions become maxims for cultural change, but this works only if they are backed up with a high level of performance and productivity. This, in fact, is the key to *every* political stand we take as Marathon Dad professionals: *we can be an agent of change toward a father-friendly work culture only if we continue to do uncompromised and outstanding professional work.*

6. He loves his children and is never afraid to show it / He loves his job and is never afraid to show it.

Our Heads: Showing our kids our love for them is one thing, but showing our love for our kids *to our fellow workers* is quite another. Likewise, showing our enthusiasm for our job to our co-workers and bosses is one thing, but showing our enthusiasm for our job *to our families* is quite another. It takes supreme confidence to resist the shaming pressures of both a jealous boss and a jealous family. It takes a great deal of self-knowledge and a strong heart to finally stop telling those old, habitual lies: *"I hate my job because it takes me away from you,"* and *"My family is a real drag because it keeps me from doing the work I really love to do."*

Just as giving up excuse-making allows us to have clearer heads and more tranquil, guilt-free hearts, giving up those lies liberates us too. We dare to love our families deeply without having to pretend that we don't love our professional lives as well. We dare to define our loyalty to our job on our own terms: "I do a damn good job and love my work, but that does not mean I have to sacrifice the rest of my life to prove it to my boss and co-workers." We get beyond the idea that we are always in a contest for what or whom we love the most. We are secure in what we *do* feel, and we really do not care what anybody else thinks we *should* feel.

Our Practices: We display our love proudly, but we do not give in to pressures for *exclusive* loyalty at either home or work. If our child says, in effect, "You can't love both your job and me. Show me you love me more!" tell him that it's not a contest, that you consider yourself very fortunate to have a life that has room for both a stimulating job and a happy, loving family life. If our boss says, in effect, "Show me your loyalty to your job by being here whenever I need you. When you sacrifice your family time, you show your loyalty to your job and there's no substitute for that," tell him that he can tell how dedicated you are to your job only by how well you do it—end of story.

Our Politics: Our mission at work is to lead our co-workers and bosses to the point where they can accept the idea that loyalty and dedication to our job is best judged by our perfor-mance at that job. Our mission at home is to lead our wives and children to the point where they can accept the idea that we can love them unconditionally while still loving our professional lives. And letting them know that loving us means loving us in our totality, as both parent and worker.

7. He never apologizes to his employer or colleagues for his loyalty to his family / He never apologizes to his family for his loyalty to his job.

Our Heads: Working fathers fall all too easily into the habit of automatic apology-making: "I'm sorry, son, I really wish I could come to the ball game this afternoon, but I've got an important meeting"; and "I'm sorry, George, I really wish I could come to that meeting this afternoon, but I promised my son I'd go to the ball game with him." Sure, it is virtuous to admit our mistakes when we make them, but when offering an apology becomes our mind-set and modus operandi at work and at home, we weaken our own confidence, make ourselves into ditherers, and encourage everyone around us to lose confidence in us. The apologies start to control us. Apology-making becomes the pathetic twin of excuse-making, another way to avoid setting priorities and feeling comfortable with them. Our task here is clear: stop it—put an end to our automatic apology-making mechanism where it begins, in our heads.

Our Practices: The way we put an end to our apology-making mind-set is the same way we finished off our excuse-making mind-set: by setting clear priorities and broadcasting them. When everybody knows what to expect, no apologies are necessary.

Our Politics: Apology-making can become a veritable culture, especially at home, where our children may start to think of us as *Dad, the Apology Maker.* This is a culture of weakness and guilt for *everyone* involved. (The kids experience guilt for feeling angry at us for disappointing them—"How can I be angry? Dad *did* apologize for missing his fifteenth ball game in a row.") Everybody wins when we stop with the apologies.

8. He is mindful of planning his family duties / He recognizes the cardinal importance of time management as a professional.

Our Heads: A persistent myth at home is that family time is fundamentally different from work time: it needs to be loose and spontaneous, so it would be "unnatural" to try to manage it. We fear treating our family like another client; we are uncomfortable with the "coldness" implicit in scheduling family time and family duties. This, of course, turns out to be a convenient alibi for not putting in enough time at home, spontaneous or otherwise: The resistance to thinking about family time in an organized way defeats it from happening at all.

Consider the analogy to marital sex by appointment: we tend to resist this system because it is unromantic, unspontaneous; reduces sex to another thing to cross off our list. However, the statistical fact is that most working couples who don't make time for sex rarely find time to do it. So the question remains: is spending *unspontaneous* time with our family better than hardly ever spending time with them at all? The answer is, of course, that we have to start managing our time for/at home as rigorously as we manage it at work.

A quite different myth prevents us from managing our time at work in a way that allows us to both get our jobs done and be hands-on fathers: we persist in believing that the *more* time we spend on the job, the better it is (and the better *we* are.) But the reality is that in a product-oriented workplace, *the quality of what gets done* is ultimately more important than simply how many hours a worker put in that week. Just as we are discovering that the concept of *Quality Time* does not cut it at home, we are discovering that the concept of *Quality Time* can be very meaningfully applied at work.

Another basic mind-set that keeps us from better parceling out our time between home and work is the one that says: *"My time at work is out of my control—I've got bosses, coworkers, and meetings determining my schedule—but at home, time is more flexible, so my wife and family can accommodate my schedule."* Nice try, but this one is at least partially wrong on both counts: first, we actually do have more control of our time at work than most of us believe (that is, if we decide to take control of it); and second, home time is getting less flexible by the minute in a house with both parents working.

Our Practices: We schedule our time at home with the same foresight, consideration, care, and communication with which we schedule our work time. This includes taking into account the time demands of all the members of the family. One key concept here is distinguishing between managing home time *efficiently* and managing it *effectively*—that is, with the focus on what will be accomplished with this particular allotted time. For example, being with your toddler at 3 P.M. may be a lot more *effective* than being with her from eight to ten at night. Again, priority-setting informs effective home-time scheduling; among other things, it keeps us from getting carried away by every "crisis" and "emergency."

Our Politics: We make our work schedules known at home and our home schedules known at work. And we prove that these schedules work by *doing both jobs effectively*. We know we are in a position to take the lead in using family-time opportunities at work or to lobby for them if they are not in place yet.

9. He acknowledges his place in the Historical Legacy of Fatherhood / He acknowledges his place in the Historical Legacy of a Professional Worker.

Our Heads: Here we get into a tricky but critical balancing act. The tradition of fatherhood clearly needs to change in the new economy, yet we still must hold on to what is good in that tradition. We start by taking a clear-eyed look at traditional fatherhood and the myths that surround it. For example, were the '50s fathers really as heartless, superficial, and uninvolved as the revisionists would have us believe? Some people out there (mostly women) argue that we have to junk everything about fatherhood we ever learned, especially from our own dads. Really? If we do that, all we'll have left as a role model is Mom. On the other hand, we recognize that motherhood has had to change too, that it has had to reinvent itself while hanging on to motherhood traditions. We need to look at the places where traditional roles have to change, but we should be careful not to throw out the baby with the bathwater. Similarly, the traditions of the work culture need to change, but we must be mindful of which of those traditions we should hang on to—for example, basic job loyalty, teamwork, responsibility, etc.

Our Practices: Our task here can be a lonely one. We stand firm against those who want us to junk every aspect of traditional fatherhood, but we also stand firm against those people (mostly men) who call our willingness to reinvent fatherhood a betrayal. We contend with revisionist views without sounding like (or becoming) pigs who do not want to change, and we demonstrate to both co-workers and family members that some changes can work to everyone's advantage.

Our Politics: We become an example of a father and a professional who embraces traditional values while seeking new ways to effect them.

10. He champions good Fatherhood with his fellow fathers / He champions Professionalism with his fellow workers.

Our Heads, Our Practices, and Our Politics: Here is where the personal becomes the political. We are Marathon Dads and proud of it. We are prepared, at work and at home, for both working fathers and working mothers to lead the way.

PART I

OUR HEADS

▼ ▼ ▼ ▼ ▼ ▼

Hurdling the Mind-sets,
Stereotypes, Guilts, and
Fears That Trip Us Up

3

A Dad Is Not a Mom

▼ ▼ ▼ ▼

Matched Set

On a hunch, I went browsing through my electronic thesaurus for verbs describing what it is that mothers and fathers do. Sure enough, mothers do *mothering*, mothers and fathers do *parenting* and *co-parenting*, but, as I suspected, there is nary a word for what fathers alone do. The word "fathering" did not make the cut for common usage.

There is a reason for that: At this particular moment in social history, the role of an actively engaged father is perceived as identical to a mother's role. An involved dad is simply a co-mother, or, as some see it, a kind of apprentice to the expert—*Mother*. In other words, Dad does the same job as Mom, just not so well.

To me, this is a colossal mistake that has led all of us—Dads and Moms alike—down a thorny path to utter confusion, overwhelming feelings of inadequacy, unnecessary marital conflict, and gross inefficiency. What it amounts to is nothing less than dumb job placement—the wrong man for the wrong job.

A *dad is not a mom*—not by talent, not by inclination, not by experience, not by nature. But what he is eminently qualified to be is A Father—to do *fathering*. And the particular constellation of talents and skills that Dad possesses for this role perfectly complements Mom's talents and skills. Dad and Mom are a matched pair—*not* an identical pair. Together, they comprise a terrific setup for sharing the business of child rearing and for offering their kids a balanced upbringing. But if Dad limps along doing his seriocomic impression of The Good Mother, he is doomed to failure—a failure that can cause serious damage to the entire family.

"I smell a rat!" I can hear a lady in the back row bellowing. "This is beginning to sound like just another male ploy for getting out of the grunge work of parenting. Some fancy psychobabble for putting us women back at the changing table dealing with cockadoodie while you're off being *real dads* giving batting tips at the Little League field."

Not so. I am the last person in the world to drum up excuses for lazy fathering or for absolving anyone from the grunge work of parenting, whether it's doing the kids' laundry or driving Emily to that highly recommended orthodontist whose office happens to be forty miles away. Nope, what I am proposing is both simpler and more complicated than that. I advocate a fair distribution of child-rearing duties, *yet one that is based on an accurate recognition of the genuine differences between good fathering and good mothering.*

These differences are primarily in the approach and the point of view that are brought to the tasks of child rearing, but they can also be differences in the actual (and fair) distribution of the tasks themselves. These stylistic differences between honest, loving, involved *fathering* and honest, loving, involved *mothering* have tremendous implications for everyone concerned—Dad, Mom, the kids, even your colleagues at work. For now, let me just assure you that a recognition of these differences makes everyone's job much easier and infinitely more fulfilling.

A Funny Thing Happened on the Way to Fathering

It is instructive to see how the notion of fathering became swallowed up by the concept of mothering. When women went back to work in record numbers as a result of economic necessity and the feminist revolution, it seemed only reasonable that men would take on more responsibilities on the home front, both with the children and with the business of running the household. As this expectation became a reality in many families, the notion of "co-parenting" was born. Raising the kids was something you did together, a set of duties and responsibilities you divvied up so that the overall workload of both wage-earning and home-running was equitably divided. The word "co-parenting" quickly devolved into "parenting"—a word that has the comforting ring of gender neutrality about it. Hey, it's the same job, and both women and men can (and should) do it, so why should it be genderized?

But here is where things got sticky. If parenting was *one* thing regardless of the gender of who did it, the only fully developed model we had for this concept was what mothers have been doing in our culture for the last millennium. Thus, Parenting equaled Mothering divided by two.

Two other factors led us, the New Involved Fathers, to seek our inspiration in Motherhood. First, when we looked to our own fathers for clues on how to behave, we did not much like what we saw. For the most part, our dads were aloof, withholding of love and approval, and stingy with their time. (Or at least it *appeared* that way, as we will see in Chapter 8: Macho Media.) That is not the kind of father we wanted to be to our own children. Our mothers, on the other hand, although at times smothering in their attentions, were more the kind of parent we aimed to be. This rejection of our own fathers as a model for parenting dovetailed nicely with the growing New Age sentiment that urged us men to get in touch with our feminine side. By liberating ourselves from the macho armor that had made our own dads so unapproachable, we could become the kinder, gentler, more sensitive parents we wished they had been. Yet in the process, it turned out that we unwittingly divested ourselves of some remarkable male characteristics that uniquely qualified us to be terrific dads.

The other major factor that led us to buy into the idea that Mothering and Parenting were one and the same thing was guilt. (This is not the last time the G word will come up as a determining influence in misguided fathering behavior, as we will see in Chapter 6: Guy Guilt.) Many of us first came to the realization that we should share parenting via guilt—via a wife who in no uncertain terms impressed on us that if she was going to hold down a job too, it was only *fair* that we pitch in at home. The more we resisted this incontrovertible moral truth, the guiltier we felt—and for good reason. So when we finally saw the light and said we wanted to do our share, we came to the task laden with guilt (not to mention burdened with legitimate feelings of inadequacy born of inexperience), making us docile, insecure students to the craft on which only She was an expert. And her lesson was simple: be a parent just like me; i.e., be a mom. We tried to comply.

To this day our guilt persists, in no small part because many of us are still not contributing fairly to the work to be done at home. But, justified or not, that guilt restrains us from following those instincts that call to us in a low voice, "Hey, pal, you're the *dad*, not the mom, remember?"

Hollywood, always busy taking the pulse of American society, quickly exploited the Dad-as-Mom phenomenon in movies like *Mr. Mom* and *Fatherhood*. But my personal favorite is the over-the-top *Mrs. Doubtfire*, in which Robin Williams plays that perennial buffoon, the immature, irresponsible father who is loads more fun than Mom. In this updated version, Mom, of course, is an overwhelmed, career-obsessed, and humorless obsessive-compulsive woman (Sally Field), who finally files for divorce when crazy Pop throws his kid a birthday party that includes a houseful of farm animals that munch on the furniture. Denied shared custody of his three children because of his irresponsibility, Williams worms his way back into his home by impersonating a proper English nanny, Mrs.

Doubtfire. Here is where the movie hits its central message: as a nanny, Williams transforms himself into the traditional idea of a perfect mother—strict, orderly, and terrific in the kitchen. In short, he becomes the partner in child rearing his wife really wants: *an old-fashioned wife*. (In case the audience happens to miss this point, the scriptwriter has Field say to Mrs. Doubtfire, "Who needs a husband when I have you?") In the end, after Field discovers that the nanny is really her husband in drag, she relents on the shared-custody issue—but she still does not want him back sharing her bed. I could not help thinking that the reason for this was that now that she finally had a fully feminized husband—a co-mom—she didn't find him sexy anymore.

Social advances have a way of going to extremes until a course correction comes along to get us back on track. If at the time when parenting qua mothering became the accepted model of behavior for dads, someone had cried foul and pleaded for a separate and distinct category of fathering, he would have been accused of gross sexism and shouted down. But now that we are at the point where we not only are *willing* to do our share of child rearing but *want* to be damned good at it, that voice can finally be heeded. Consider the course on its way to being corrected. Henceforth, in this book at least, the word "parenting" shall be banned. What we are interested in is good *fathering*.

Do You Want to Play Catch or Talk About It?

There is a telling moment near the end of the film *Field of Dreams,* when the ghost of the hero's long-estranged father appears on the baseball field that the hero has built behind his house. The hero's wife, sensing that this is a unique opportunity for father and son to resolve some serious unfinished business, retires to their farmhouse with the encouraging parting words, "You two have a lot to talk about." Yet when father and son try to converse, the attempt is stilted and awkward;

nothing of consequence is said. Then, as the father starts to walk away, the hero calls to him, "Wanna play some catch, Dad?" Yes, that is precisely what the father would like to do. Wordlessly throwing a baseball back and forth, father and son connect in a way that spoken words could never do for them. The shared physical activity is at once a metaphor for and a resolution of their serious unfinished business.

This scene captures in a nutshell one of the many essential differences between dads and moms, between fathering and mothering. In general (although, of course, with vast amounts of individual variation), dads seek nonverbal ways to be intimate with their children, while moms tend to favor direct verbal intimacy—they want to talk about it. But lo and behold, it turns out that our children get something important from *both* forms of intimacy. A wordless game of catch with your son or daughter can provide you and your child with a personal connection that no heart-to-heart talk can; and a mother's heart-to-heart talk with her son or daughter can provide them with a personal connection that no game of catch can. *Neither approach is superior to the other.* In fact, the *combination* of both approaches enriches the child's life and promotes his or her personal growth more than a steady diet of either one of them. As we will see, this principle of the *complementarity* of fathering and mothering is vastly significant and far-reaching. Strictly from the child's point of view, it is the most important reason why Dad should never even try to be a mom—he would be depriving his child of a nurturing balance.

It is time we took a good look at these modal differences between dads and moms, between fathering and mothering. But first, I have to respond to that bearded fellow with the open notebook in the front row who has been wagging his hand at me for the past five minutes.

"What kind of differences are you talking about?" he wants

to know. "Historical differences? Traditional differences? Cultural differences? *Biological* differences? Those are all just artifacts, man. Constructs that get handed down to us like tattered baggage. Get with the program—we are free to be whomever we want, to be whatever kind of parent we want to be. So don't give me this To-Thine-Own-Gender-Be-True bullshit!"

This fellow is right, of course—these differences between fathering and mothering styles *are* artifacts. And, indeed, they have been handed down to us from generation to generation, for the most part rather uncritically. But nonetheless, we are who we are because of who we have been. The fact is that these different styles are the result of our *evolved adaptations* to the special requirements of the weak and needy human child. No, we should not embrace these differences uncritically, but it does make damned good sense for both Dad and Mom to go with their respective strengths. Among other reasons, *not* to do so is simply to invite gross inefficiency.

Let me give you an example of the way one fathering/mothering adaptation evolved. Historically (and in primitive societies), men were generally assigned the task of providing physical security on the perimeter of the household or community. (The main reason for this, incidentally, was not the male's superior strength, but because he was more expendable. To ensure the survival of the community, you need more wombs than gonads; one male can impregnate more than one woman, while, of course, one woman cannot simultaneously gestate several men's babies.) But given this task of guarding the perimeter, fathers developed the skills for physical defense and protection, which, in turn, they passed on to their sons. In the meantime, inside the protected zone, the female saw to developing other kinds of security for the children—the kinds that in modern terms would be called *emotional* security.

Although these differences in providing the child with security have gone through myriad changes and historical adaptations, at base they are still with us. Yes, women are out there in the world competing just the way we do, and no, Bearded One, I would not have it differently—I do not advocate women staying at home by the hearth. Nonetheless, whether by nature or nurture or some incalculable combination of the two, men, in general, remain more competent at bestowing the child with and instructing the child in the techniques of physical security. In today's world, that means providing the child with skills for dealing with the slings and arrows of the outside world—showing and teaching how to compete and survive out there. And women, in general, are more competent at bestowing the child with and instructing the child in the techniques of emotional security. Today, that means providing the child with a strong sense of selfhood, teaching the child how to develop and maintain a strong personal identity. *Both* are necessary for successfully nurturing a child. So isn't it grand that we have specialists in each area to do that nurturing?

Obviously, a father's and mother's areas of speciality overlap—more so today than ever before. Today's father is both able to *and* wants to come in from the perimeter to participate in the child's emotional development. But the reality remains that this man—yes, *this cultural artifact*—is probably more in touch with the fact that the perimeter cannot be left unprotected.

Okay, let's lay out these basic differences between the adaptive strengths of dads and moms.

DAD	MOM
Play & work more physical, more contact. Seeks nonverbal ways to be intimate. **"Let's play catch!"**	Play & work more relational, more cerebral. Seeks direct verbal intimacy. **"Let's talk."**

DAD	MOM
Greater focus on preparing the child to compete, succeed, and take on responsibility. Helps define what the world expects and what the child is up against. **"Fight the good fight!"**	Tends to downplay competition for the well-being of the child, to protect his/her emotional security. Helps define the child's individuality based on what she considers a realistic appraisal of child's capabilities. **"Do the best you can and enjoy it!"**
Teaches crisis management as a survival skill. **"Be prepared for the unexpected!"**	Teaches the order and routines of daily life. **"Be prepared for tomorrow!"**
Encourages risk-taking—physically, intellectually, and emotionally. **"Go for it! Reach for the stars!"**	Encourages caution, safety, and weighing of options. **"Watch your step!"**
Emotionally impulsive, both more playful and more likely to show anger directly. Less likely to suffer hurt feelings as a result of interaction with child. **"That pisses me off, Joey!"**	Tends to moderate and hide anger to protect child from her emotions. More likely to suffer hurt feelings as a result of an interaction with child. **"We have to sit down and talk about this, Joey."**
More aggressive, confrontational disciplinarian. **The "Look"**	More likely to withdraw emotionally as a form of punishment. **The Silent Treatment**
More focused on child's social standing. Encourages both teamwork and leadership. **"Be a team player, but stake out your territory!"**	More concerned with child's internal sense of self. Encourages personal pride and self-reliance. **"Be yourself and the rest will take care of itself."**
Encourages and prepares child for flight from the nest. **"Goodbye and good luck, pal!"**	Tends to hold on to child until she is absolutely sure child can make it on his/her own. **"We're always here for you, sweetie."**

4

Home Improvements

▼ ▼ ▼ ▼

What Difference Does the Difference Make?

"Let's Play Catch!" / "Let's Talk."

Nowhere is the contrast between fathering and mothering styles more evident than in the realm of communication. It starts early. Studies show that when mothers interact with their young children, they are much more likely to keep a dialogue alive by pressing the child with questions, prodding him to speak in complete sentences, urging him to get out everything he has to say. Fathers, on the other hand, are much more likely to ask their kids for clarification with an open-ended "What?" If that doesn't clear matters up, Dad will probably drop it and move on to something else. Further, Dad is twice as likely to ignore his child's pronouncements than Mom is. One outcome of this is that young children very quickly learn how to become clearer communicators when talking with Mom.

The logical conclusion we are tempted to draw from this statistic is that Dad stinks at parent-child communication, that he needs some serious retraining if he is going to be a good and caring father—in short, that he should try to be more like Mom in this area. But there is a surprising other half to this picture: the same studies show that Dad's seemingly bluff communication style challenges the child to make adjustments when talking with him. By implicitly expecting his child to communicate in a more adult manner, Dad is preparing the child for the world outside the nest where no one will be there to patiently prod her/him for verbal clarity. Dad is once again performing his role of training his child for independence. And Dad *and* Mom are once again working in tandem for the best possible result: the child learns verbal explication from Mom and verbal self-reliance from Dad.

Obviously, this is not an alibi for a dad who ignores his child completely, who does not pay attention to his son or daughter—there is no excuse for that. The fact is everything we do—verbal and otherwise—communicates a message to our children, and ignoring a child can, unhappily, speak volumes to him. But on the positive side, as that scene from *Field of Dreams* movingly illustrates, there are other effective ways to communicate with and intimately relate to a child than simply talking.

I am reminded of a thirty-six-year-old father, Jack, whom I saw in my practice. Jack was deeply disturbed by the chasm he felt had grown between him and his only child, a ten-year-old daughter named Autumn.

"Joan [his wife] keeps urging me to sit down and talk with Autumn, but it's always a bust," Jack told me. "It's like we're on totally different wavelengths. Joan says it's because I'm always rushing Autumn, that I don't take my time with her. I try—God, how I try!—but it's still no go. I feel like a failure as a father."

Jack went on to say that he had always prided himself on being a good communicator, that in his work as a lawyer he was known for having a talent for clear and precise communication.

"But with Autumn, I couldn't do any worse if I were struck dumb," he told me miserably.

"Actually, being struck dumb sounds like a terrific idea to me," I said. "Try skipping the words for a bit. I get the impression that your wife handles that part pretty well on her own."

As we explored Jack's relationship with his daughter further, I learned that Autumn often liked to play alone in her room with doll miniatures. I also found out that one of Jack's favorite pastimes—though long neglected—was woodworking. It seemed like a match made in heaven.

"Maybe you two should build a dollhouse together," I suggested. "And remember, the less talk the better."

Jack thought it was worth a try.

The dollhouse project was slow getting off the ground— Autumn did not much like the prospect of spending all that time with her father—but once they got started, there was no stopping them. It became something they both looked forward to; at times they would rush through dinner to get to it (to Joan's occasional annoyance.) Jack kept to the idea of minimal talk, only a brief "Pass the glue" or "What do you think, red or purple?" In truth, Jack discovered that he tremendously enjoyed these periods of long silences after all the yakking he did at work. And Autumn took pleasure in the silent activity too, just as she did alone in her room after a busy social day at school and after her long (and enjoyable) conversations with her mother. It turned out that in this way she was very much her father's daughter.

One day, near the end of therapy, Jack came into my office beaming. Just last evening as they were putting the final touches on the dollhouse, Autumn had become lethargic and visibly unhappy. Without thinking about it, Jack had murmured, "Something wrong?" Starting to cry, Autumn had blurted, "It's all over!"

"She was thinking that was it, that we wouldn't be spending any more time together," Jack told me. "But I gave her a hug

and said, 'So what should we do next? Some doll furniture?
A jewelry box?' "

They had happily discussed the possibilities for close to an
hour, finally settling on a birdhouse. Jack says it was the long-
est, most engaged, and, in its way, most intimate conversation
he had ever had with his daughter.

I have to admit that at one point in my career I probably
would have urged Jack straightaway to take a hard look at how
he was speaking to his child, that he would probably see that
he was talking down to her, expecting her to be as clear as a
lawyer. I might even have pressed him to take a cue from his
wife so as to improve his communication skills with his daughter. But by the time Jack first walked into my office, I had
learned a thing or two about the differences in the communication styles of fathers and mothers, and how the synergy
between them could afford the child the best of all possible
worlds. I like to believe that Jack benefited from that knowledge. Not only did he create a channel of intimacy with his
daughter, but Autumn came away from the experience with
a new skill—woodworking. Dad had opened up a new and
nontraditional possibility for her in the world.

"Fight the Good Fight!" / "Do the Best You Can and Enjoy It!"

When I was a kid, almost every Saturday morning my father
and I used to race each other from our driveway all the way to
the end of our street. My dad had been a schoolboy basketball
champion and all-around athlete with a dozen interscholastic
medals to prove it. He invariably beat me.

There were times when I felt so frustrated by losing that I
had to hold back tears. And more than once I fantasized Pop
tripping on a stray milk bottle and flopping down on the pave-
ment as I trotted by triumphantly. That never happened.

Many years later, my brother told me that he had once
overheard my mother berate my father for always beating me

at our Saturday marathons. Mom had argued that he was making me feel bad, and worse, that he was making me so competitive that all the joy of running was being drained out of me. He had countered that he was training me to dig deep, to try to go beyond my wildest expectations for myself. "That's what makes champions!" my brother remembers him adamantly professing.

But the story does not end there.

One Saturday morning when I was thirteen and my father had just entered his forties, I finally beat him—only by a couple of strides, but, by God, I beat him, beat him fair and square. I remember looking back at him exultantly.

"Good for you, Johnny!" he called to me. But on his face I saw something other than pride in his son's triumph—Dad's face belied the pain of his own defeat. In some way I wish he had been able to transcend that feeling, or at the very least to have tried harder to hide it from me.

I often find myself referring back to this episode when I think about this second categorical difference between fathering and mothering—*preparing the child to compete and succeed* vs. *downplaying competition to protect the child's emotional security.*

True to his generation, my dad was not one to easily show pride in and affection to his children, and I am convinced that my siblings and I have been affected by this. We sometimes came away feeling that we could never be good enough for him, that we were never worthy of his unconditional love. This undoubtably left its mark on us. Yet when I think about those Saturday morning races, I have to remind myself that I did indeed learn how to "dig deep" from my father and I think that has served me well in life. It has brought me satisfactions and a sense of achievement that I never would have reached for if he had not instilled this ethic in me. And the truth is, if my mother had prevailed and, say, my father had thrown the races so I could win once in a while, I might not have had what it takes to garner those satisfactions later in my life.

Still, I am also convinced that our Dads could have achieved the same goal with us *while being more supportive and loving in the bargain*. They could have made a greater effort to get out of themselves, to leave their own egos behind when they were training us to push ourselves beyond our wildest expectations. That is what we must try very hard to do with our own children.

The point I want to make here is that, like generations of fathers before us, we have an aptitude for pushing our children to compete and succeed, while in general, the mothers of our children retain the countervailing aptitude for protecting our children from feelings of defeat and inadequacy. And once again, these two very different aptitudes can successfully complement each other. But that does not mean that we, as a more involved and sensitive generation of fathers, cannot push our children to succeed *with greater compassion than our own fathers did*.

Am I suddenly pleading for a feminization of the father's role? I don't think so. I, for one, do not feel feminized or alienated by feeling and showing compassion to my kids. Yet by the same token I know that I *would* feel untrue to my innate fathering instincts if I were to force myself to desist from urging my children to compete, from preparing them for the rough-and-tumble of the outside world.

In my town there is a private day school that advocates a philosophy of strict noncompetitiveness. To this end, the teachers do not give their students grades or class rankings; similarly, their athletic program is designed to maximize the pleasure of movement while minimizing the stress of competition. To me, there is something decidedly one-sided about this setup—it strikes me as totally feminized. (In general, I find early education to be overly feminized as a result of the fact that ninety-plus percent of K–6 teachers are women—but more later as to what I think we fathers can do about that.) This past summer the parents of a student at this noncompetitive school approached me in my capacity as coach of the local boys' soccer team. They told me that their son, Erik, played soccer at his school and wanted to join the town team. I said that I was happy to have him on board.

At our first practice I observed two things about Erik: he had natural athletic talent and he put absolutely no effort or concentration into playing ball. One way of looking at this would be to say that Erik was supremely noncompetitive; another way of looking at it would be to say that he was supremely lazy. I subscribed to the latter evaluation. Also, I believed that Erik would enjoy playing soccer a hell of a lot more if he put some heart into it.

I pushed him. He resisted. I pushed him harder. He got kicked in the shins and was on the brink of crying. Erik's mother came to see me; she patiently explained her son's school philosophy to me. I, in turn, explained to her that I considered soccer to be a competitive sport, but that there were any number of other, noncompetitive sports available to Erik, like hiking and swimming. At this point, Erik—who had been loitering a few feet away from us—declared that he wanted to keep playing soccer on the team.

That, as they say, was the turnaround moment. From then on, Erik played his heart out. He received innumerable more kicks in the shin and a few other body parts, and he inflicted a few of his own; he always played fairly and in a sportsman-like manner, but he always played hard. At the end of the summer, there was no doubt about it: Erik felt good about himself and it was reflected in everything about him—his posture, his face, his confidence, his companionableness.

But for me, something equally as interesting as Erik's transformation had happened—his mother stopped coming to our games so frequently, while his father, who initially had shown up only sporadically, began coming to every one of them and cheering the boys on. Up until that summer, Erik's dad, I believe, had been trying to be a mom; but Erik already had a mom, and a perfectly capable one. By going along with the program of the boy's feminized school, Erik's dad had been denying something in himself—something I am pretty sure that he, as a father, intuitively felt that his child needed. I am convinced that his intuitions were absolutely right in this instance.

"Be Prepared for the Unexpected!" / "Be Prepared for Tomorrow!'

This difference in fathering and mothering has its roots in the guarding-the-perimeter paradigm: Dad is the expert on the unforeseen; Mom is the expert on the current scene. Dad, despite his predilection for risk-taking, is more likely to be the parent who is on the lookout for people who might take advantage of his children; he warns his daughter or son to be vigilant of the smiling smooth talkers and wily deceivers who lurk beyond the perimeter. And Mom, despite her predilection for caution, is more apt to encourage trust with others, to teach her children the ways of an orderly existence that by its very nature eschews unexpected people and events. Again, an effective combo, especially when paired with the risk-taking/caution antinomies.

But these differences in approach can easily lead to major dissension between Mom and Dad, especially in the realm of how to respond to authority. Dad is usually far less likely to trust an authority's pronouncements when it impinges on his children than Mom is.

Last year a couple, Bob and Carla, came to see me in the throes of a very serious conflict about their eight-year-old son, Paul, who had what is today euphemistically called a "behavior problem" at school. Paul, it seemed, could not sit still in the classroom, did not pay attention to instructions, and was given to inappropriate outbursts. He was also, according to his father, a kid with a good heart, a lively imagination, and an indomitable spirit.

Paul's third-grade teacher, a seasoned educator in her fifties, had sent Paul to the school psychologist for evaluation. This expert's diagnosis was that Paul suffered from Attention Deficit Disorder; he recommended that the boy be put on Ritalin, a stimulant drug that "focuses" children suffering from this syndrome. In a meeting with Bob and Carla, the psychologist informed them that once the drug kicked in and Paul's disorder was corrected, the boy would be a new person—a vastly improved student, a happier kid with greater self-esteem who would get along better with teachers and peers alike. Carla was convinced. Bob was not.

"I'll tell you what worries me about it," Bob told me, obviously worked up. "It sounds like social control to me. Paul's a problem for them in the classroom, so let's drug him. It's a quick fix for *their* problem, not his. I don't like it one bit."

"I just want my boy to be happier!" Carla cried, her eyes tearing up. "He is miserable at the end of every day. He has to stand in the hall or go to the principal's office—he failed another quiz and was told he's going to be left back. I just can't stand to see him suffer anymore. If the Ritalin will help, I say try it."

"But I don't trust them!" Bob blurted.

"You don't trust anybody!" Carla retorted. "Listen, I'm the one who picks him up at school every day. I think I know what's right for Pauly better than you do!"

This, of course, was Carla's trump card, her version of Mother Knows Best. And indeed, she did have more *firsthand* information about how her son was affected by his school day. But I could see that Carla's words had the effect of making Bob less secure in his position. He felt guilty about what seemed to be an obvious inequity in their child-care arrangement—Carla had arranged her work schedule so that she could pick up Paul every day after school; Bob had not.

"There's just got to be a better way," he murmured, already a hint of defeat in his tone.

Truth to tell, I was not sure where I myself stood on the issue of giving Paul Ritalin. On the one hand, I do believe it is overprescribed, often for the very reason that Bob suspected—social control; but on the other hand, I personally have seen a great many "problem children" whose entire lives radically improved after being on the drug. Furthermore, it was clear to me that Carla and Bob each wanted what they thought was best for their child; I did not detect any motive in either of them other than their son's best interest. What I was witnessing was a classic instance of a familiar difference in approach between fathering and mothering: Dad was vigilant and suspicious of authority when it came to his child; Mom was overwhelmingly concerned with her child's emotional well-being, even if that meant accommodating the system.

But understanding that difference did not in itself go very far in helping me resolve their conflict. The way I thought I could help was by showing Bob and Carla how they might be able to reach a resolution without either of them abandoning their respective strengths as the father and mother. To get there, Bob would have to feel that he was an equal partner in the decision; otherwise, he would always believe he had failed his son as a father, or perhaps more to the point, as a second-rate mother.

I asked them to delay for a month the decision of whether or not to put Paul on Ritalin. In the meantime, I urged Bob to arrange his life so he could pick up his son at school on alternate days—at least until the decision was resolved; if he was constantly fighting his guilt, he would be endlessly insecure in his position. What's more, he might indeed learn something about how school affected his son by being there on the spot as Carla had been. Finally, I said this to Bob:

"You said you thought there must be a better way of dealing with Paul's problem. Why don't you see what you can come up with?"

Bob was understandably reluctant to follow my advice, primarily because his place of work, an advertising agency, did not look charitably on men who left the office early to pick up their children at school. In short, Bob had hit Collision Point #1 on Marathon Dad's obstacle course: should he dodge his responsibilities to his child in order to stay on course at work, or should he hurdle the male stereotype of a "fully committed worker" to stay on course as a dad? Never an easy decision for the best of us. But as we will see throughout this book, we must always be alert to those times when jumping the hurdle of tradition is the only way to go. Bob was a man who knew his value at work; what was in question was his value as a father. He chose to pick up his son at school.

I am very happy to report that Bob and Carla resolved their conflict in the best possible way. By picking up his son at school, Bob not only observed how miserable his son was there, he discovered that this school was far more rigid than he had ever thought it to be. He also noticed something else: all of the grammar-school teachers were women. This observation, combined with the recently learned fact that some eighty percent of children diagnosed with Attention Deficit Disorder are boys, led Bob to the conclusion that before he allowed Paul to be put on Ritalin, he wanted to find a different school for him, one that was more active-boy-friendly—preferably a school that had more male teachers in the lower grades. In typical male tradition, Bob thoroughly researched the options and found such a school. When Bob and Carla met with this school's principal, the school psychologist was present; he said that Ritalin was a last resort there, an option they sometimes recommended, but not until they had tried other strategies, including alternating rough-and-tumble exercise with academic lessons throughout the school day.

At last report, Paul was doing well at this school, still not the best of students, but a much happier boy without the aid of Ritalin. Both Carla and Bob are very pleased. In a session

I had alone with Bob at the end of our work together, he said, "Thanks for helping me follow my instincts."

"No problem," I replied. "They were *your* instincts."

I imagine there are some of you out there who are thinking, All well and good, but this fellow Bob ended up with more work to do, not less—plus he had to risk alienating his employers. I thought we were learning how to make our jobs as fathers easier, not harder.

Ultimately, I believe Bob's job as a father *was* made easier. Yes, he had to put in more time at it, at least temporarily; but in the end, by doing what he thought was right and by doing *what he was good at as a father*, he was less stressed, less guilty, and far more energized than if he had simply abandoned his role. I should add that by putting in some extra time on weekends, he was able to more than fulfill his work commitments; his job has remained as secure as ever.

"Go for It!" / "Watch Your Step!"

By now you have probably realized that Dad's propensity for being on guard against anyone who might take unfair advantage of his child is not at odds with his propensity for urging his child to take risks; actually, these are corollaries. If you are going to urge your child to go for it, to go out into the world and take the chances which may bring great rewards, you will also want the child to be well prepared for all the pitfalls out there—it's part of the same package.

Like other stylistic differences between fathering and mothering, the *encouraging risk-taking/encouraging caution* dyad holds the potential for some out-and-out conflict between Dad and Mom. But what I want to stress here is that such a conflict—even if it gets damned loud—is not necessarily a bad thing, for either your child or your marriage. As we will see when we explore the notion of Complementarity, kids often get something quite valuable out of the contrast between

Dad's and Mom's approaches and values, even if this contrast surfaces as an argument between them. It gives the children options to choose from. The fact is, kids do not much like the idea of Dad and Mom always agreeing on everything with regard to them, of Mom and Dad being One Thing. And as to your marriage, I'll just say here that as a psychotherapist, I have always subscribed to the belief that, nine times out of ten, the *expression* of honest differences between partners is healthier than the *repression* of those differences.

This *dad/mom, risk/caution* difference in style often surfaces early in the child-rearing process. Dad encourages Junior to ride his bicycle solo without the aid of training wheels; Mom encourages Junior to wait until he has bicycle riding absolutely down pat before he tries his first solo flight; Junior hears both sides and makes up his own mind.

One neat illustration of this phenomenon happened right up the street from me. One winter day, neighbors took their four-year-old, nonidentical girl twins over to a gradual slope where the younger kids go sledding. After taking the girls down the hill with him in a sled a few times, Dad wanted to put his daughters, one at a time, on a plastic "saucer" and let them try it alone. Mom protested: too dangerous. Dad countered that it was perfectly safe, the hill was not steep, the snow was soft, and the worst that could happen was that they would tumble in the snow. But Mom insisted that the speed alone could traumatize them. I watched from the sidelines, wondering how this familiar mom/dad conflict would play out. I noticed that, rather than being upset by their parents' rapidly escalating argument, the girls seemed fascinated, almost bemused. Then, almost simultaneously, one of the twins announced that she did not want to sled alone in a saucer, while the other announced that she *did* want to.

Some therapists would interpret the twins' response as their way of working out their parents' conflict for them. Perhaps, but what was most significant to me was that each of these girls felt secure in her decision whether to sled or not to sled.

They had listened to the pros and cons of risk-taking and made up their own minds about which course they wanted to take. I don't believe that either twin felt that she had betrayed or been loyal to her dad or mom; rather, I believe each girl felt that she had an ally in her decision.

As children grow older, the idea of whether to take a risk or follow a more cautious route branches into intellectual and emotional areas of their lives. Should they take the risk of choosing the harder course? Should they take the risk of staking out a bold and original position on a social issue at school? Should they take the risk of asking that hot-looking hunk to the prom? Dad, in general, will argue for reaching for the stars; Mom, for taking your time, weighing your options, and watching your step. I cannot imagine a more balanced set of options being set out for the child whom they are bringing up together.

Once again, Marathon Dad's guiding principle of *"As you are at work, so shall you be at home—and vice versa"* comes into play. If, at home, the Dad-Who-Is-Trying-to-Be-a-Mom curbs his instinct to encourage his children to take risks, he will inevitably (if unwittingly) find himself curbing this same instinct on the job. Studies show that risk-taking in business is a distinctively male aptitude, yet currently this strength is on the wane. It is my belief that this has contributed to the *overfeminization* of some workplaces—those offices where risk-taking tends to be constrained, often to the detriment of business goals.

"That Pisses Me Off, Joey!" / "We Have to Sit Down and Talk About This, Joey."

I have a friend who rarely saw her father when she was growing up (he was an itinerant consultant), but who carries a cherished memory of him that she often plays back in her mind.

"Whenever he was home and it started raining outside, Dad

would say to me, 'Hey, kiddo, let's go for a walk in the rain.' My mother would always try to stop us—she was afraid I'd come down with pneumonia or something—but out we'd go into the rain. No hat, no umbrella—we'd just walk and walk, getting sopped, not really talking much but laughing a lot. I never felt so alive as when we took those rainy-day walks. And I never loved him so much as then either."

Dads, in general, are apt to be more impulsive with their children than moms are, whether that impulse leads to a walk in the rain, a spontaneous purchase (which is not in the budget Mom oversees), or an outburst of emotion—including anger. Once more this can lead to conflict between Dad and Mom. After all, Mom is most likely the one who has to deal with the wet clothes when Dad and daughter come in from the rain (not fair!); Mom is most likely the one to wrestle with the household budget after Dad has spontaneously bought his son a pair of top-of-the-line ice skates (not fair!); and Mom is the one who most often ends up having to comfort the child after Dad blows his top (probably fair in the grand complementary scheme of things).

Here again, we have to be careful not to throw out unique fathering qualities along with unfair sexist behavior. For example, there is no reason why Dad (*and* daughter) should not deal with those wet clothes themselves; and if Dad overdoes it with one of his spur-of-the-moment purchases, he can try to make up for it out of his own personal budget. *But it would be a real shame if Dad became cowed into thoroughly repressing his impulsive instincts for the sake of becoming a "better parent," i.e., more momlike.*

For one thing, Dad's impulsivity is more fun. Now, I know there are scores of working moms out there who have had it up to here with Barrels-of-Fun Dad, just as Sally Fields had had it with Robin Williams at the beginning of *Mrs. Doubtfire*. This dad is totally irresponsible, immature, not to mention guilty of that most unpardonable of crimes, being the front-runner in the Favorite Parent Sweepstakes—while old responsible Mom, who does most of the grunt work of child rearing, comes in a distant second. But, I repeat, there is no reason why a conscientious dad cannot be impulsive *and* responsible (put the clothes in the dryer) at the same time. And leave us not underestimate the value of fun.

In these days of parents who are highly ambitious for their children, there is a tendency to see every experience the child has as a potential lesson that can make him a better, more "marketable" person. On the surface, a joyful walk in the rain does not qualify for this category (although, as you will see below, I believe that in part it does qualify). But even if it does not, what in the name of God is wrong with having some plain old-fashioned, noninstructive fun with your kid? Not every experience with your child has to be a lesson. Some experiences are just that—experiences. Childhood experiences are what childhood is made up of, so shouldn't a good many of them be fun? Providing such experiences happens to be part of what good fathering is all about.

And in a very real sense, those spontaneous walks in the rain *are* instructive. Probably the most underestimated aspect of fathering and mothering is in the *modeling* we provide for our children. These are not lessons where we say, "Here's the right way to do it, kid"; *these are the lessons we teach by the examples we set.* In every study of child development that I know of, the lessons of modeling have a more pronounced and long-lasting effect on the kind of person the child becomes than any parental program of direct tutorial. "Do as I say, not as I do" never did and never will cut it with children. In the final tally, kids are much more likely to do as you *do*. This is particularly true in the arena of moral behavior and "ways of being" in the world. And that is why it is particularly important for Dad to unapologetically be *himself*—because a child with an unauthentic model is a child with no model at all.

So what lesson of modeling does a walk in the rain offer your child?

It teaches her (or him) to try new things, to every so often go with her impulses, to give herself to experiences of the unplanned and unexpected—*to have fun!* In a world in which stress is rapidly becoming the chief cause of ill health and in which fun is in increasingly short supply, this may very well be one of the most important lessons you will ever impart to your child. Furthermore, coupled with Dad's prod to risk-taking, this example of spontaneity offers the child an option of behavior that can have profound implications for every aspect of his life, including his eventual approach to work in his profession. The professional who is comfortable with his spontaneous impulses just may have a leg up when it comes to making quick, work-related decisions when they are needed.

But not every spontaneous performance by Dad is fun for the child. Dads, in general, are more likely than moms to show their unvarnished anger, sudden and loud and scary. Do not think for a moment that I condone abuse by Dad, verbal, physical, or otherwise; there is no excuse for the sustained, mean-spirited wounding of any child. Yet there is a sense in which the concept of abuse has become so stretched and overly feminized that in some families it has come to mean that Dad should *always* suppress his anger.

This, I believe, is a serious mistake for everyone concerned. There is all the difference in the world between the dad who screams, "That pisses me off, Joey!" (when for the third time in a row Joey turns up his cd player full blast while you are trying to read a report) and the dad who gives him the back of his hand—or even the dad who shouts, "You're an idiot, Joey! Only an idiot would listen to crap like that!" The first is an honest reaction that makes a point without doing serious damage; the second and third can do serious damage to your child and to your relationship with him. There is all the difference in the world between (loudly) criticizing what your child *has done* and *demeaning who he is.* Once again, the point is not to throw out your fathering instincts along with any tendency you may have to be wounding to your child. Male griz-zlies are known to eat their young—now, I call that inappropriate behavior for human fathers. But that does not mean we should abandon our growl. Don't *throw out* all your spontaneous anger, *just keep it from being unnecessarily dam-aging*. This is not always an easy distinction to make or follow, especially in the heat of the moment, but it is well within our reach if we are conscious of it.

And what is the value in showing your anger to your child, you may wonder?

For starters, showing anger remains a legitimate way to teach your child what you feel is acceptable and unacceptable behavior (not everything in this area can be conveyed by *talk-ing* about it, despite the current feminized tendency other-wise). But perhaps even more importantly, a father who shows his anger provides his child with an emotional model, one that in the long run may make for a more emotionally healthy child. "Anger is okay," his modeling says. "Feel it, get it out, and get on with your life."

And let us not forget the balancing effect of Complementar-ity here. In my experience, the oft-played scenario of Dad blowing his top over his child's misbehavior, followed by Mom comforting the chagrined child, is *not* necessarily the confus-ing, destructive force we postmodern parents have been led to believe. It conveys lessons that *both* are needed for a healthy upbringing: "Joey, you did, indeed, do something deserving of Dad's pissed-offness. But that doesn't mean you are undeserv-ing of love and comfort."

The danger here, of course, is that Dad can become totally associated with the negative side of this dyad, while Mom becomes totally associated with the positive side—the old par-adigm of Dad is feared and Mom is cherished for her warmth and comfort. But things do not have to turn out this way. If Dad blows his top and *then quickly gets over it* (something we *do* have a talent for), the child will soon learn that Dad's love has not been permanently withdrawn, that Dad wants to get on with their relationship—but he sure as hell wants some adjustments in the child's behavior too.

It is no secret that many of today's children suffer the handicap of being so spoiled by their parents that they lack a compass for their behavior, a handicap that will put them at a severe disadvantage in the outside world. And it is my belief that a major contribution to this New Spoiled Child Syndrome are those dads who become moms—dads who suppress their justified and sincerely felt anger in favor of long, reasonable, momlike talks with the child about his misbehavior.

Just the other day in a restaurant, I saw a domestic scene unfold that I must have seen transpire dozens of times in recent years. An attractive, upscale dad and mom were sitting at a table near ours with their Gap-dressed three-year-old son. No sooner had the bread basket arrived than this little fellow grabbed a muffin, took a bite, and, apparently unhappy with his choice, tossed the rest of the muffin onto the floor. Dad, I could see already, was fighting to control his anger—an internal contest I am sure he engaged in daily, if not hourly. The most Dad could allow himself to do was to very gingerly remove the bread basket from his son's reach. The boy responded by screaming that he wanted the basket and he wanted it now. Here Mom went into high gear: she proffered the basket back to the boy while explaining to him in reasonable tones that bread was for eating, not for throwing. I even overheard her say something to the effect that in ancient times bread was so valued that it was known as the staff of life. Very educational. All the while, Dad kept sitting on his anger.

Should Dad have followed his instincts and blown his top, risking a scene and embarrassment all around? I believe so. Although the fact of the matter is Dad's controlled outburst was so long overdue that neither child nor mate might have known what to make of it. Dad should have blown his top on as many justified previous occasions as it would have taken for this scene never to have happened in the first place. The boy would have known better than to incur Dad's wrath.

Anger, yes; abuse, no. That hardly seems like an impossible principle for Dad to follow.

An interesting corollary to Dad's propensity for spontaneous anger is his greater tolerance of the *child's* anger. Dad is less likely than Mom to suffer and sustain hurt feelings as a result of his interactions with his child; he knows he gets over his own anger and back to loving his kid, so he assumes his kid will probably go through a similar process. Every parent—moms and dads alike—abhor those inevitable moments when the frustrated child screams, "I hate you!" God, how they sting! But if *both* parents live in so much fear of these moments that they do everything they can to avoid them—which means desisting from virtually all discipline—the entire family is in trouble. Once again, Dad's proclivity toward being better able to accept his child's outbursts puts him in a position to keep his child from becoming a little tyrant. Further, Dad is modeling for his child again and the lesson is crucial: "As I get over your outbursts of anger, so you can get over mine."

The "Look" / The Silent Treatment

How many among you cannot remember that fear-inspiring look that Dad drilled at you when you had crossed the boundaries of acceptable behavior? "The Skunk," one of my friends called it. "The Evil Eye" was another's name for it. But we all knew that look—it was stern and frightening and made us wish to God that we had never done whatever it was that we had done to deserve it. I even remember once asking one of my brothers how Dad had learned how to do "The Look" so well.

"From Grampa," came the reply.

My brother was right. "The Look" is one of those skills that has been passed down from generation to generation of fathers for as long as any of us can remember.

But The Look is in scarce supply these days. Clearly, the

most disturbing reason why is because so few dads are at home with their children to give them The Look. (Fathers have literally abandoned their kids to the point where sixty percent of children in America today grow up without one around.) Still, for those of us who not only are at home but want to be deeply involved in raising our children, The Look is under threat of extinction by those forces that would have us behave more like milder, unthreatening moms. And giving up The Look should not be done lightly. Along with our spontaneous flashes of disapproving anger, it remains a potent fathering tool for invoking discipline.

When it comes to handing out discipline, dads are more likely than moms to be aggressive and confrontational with their children. They shoot The Look, they give The Talking-to, they create and invoke a lesson-giving punishment. Moms, on the other hand, are more likely to deal with a misbehaving child with standardized punishments (like, "Go to your room," or "Sit on the stairs until you are ready to be a good boy"), withdrawal, silence, and other subtly guilt-inducing behavior. Each style works; and once again, combined, they are the best setup for a child to learn the limits of acceptable behavior.

One day when I was in second grade, instead of coming directly home after school as was the house rule, I took off with a friend to explore the railroad tracks that cut behind town. Fortunately, nothing untoward happened to us, but I did not return home until a good two hours after I was expected. My mother was beside herself with worry; she had already phoned half the neighborhood and was on the brink of calling the police. When I walked in the kitchen door, scruffy and hungry, she gazed at me for only a fraction of a second, then abruptly turned her back to me and ordered me up to my room to "wait until your father gets home!"

I remember crouching at the window, waiting for Dad's old Plymouth to round the corner, my stomach in such turmoil that every trace of hunger vanished. Behind me, two of my brothers speculated on what Dad would do to me. The consensus was that I would be grounded to the backyard for a month, which meant, among other things, that I would miss the Memorial Day parade.

The Plymouth arrived. I ducked down from the window, my heart beating wildly. I offered up a desperate prayer. "Please, God, let him be easy on me and I swear on all things holy that I won't even look at a railroad track again." I listened intently as I heard Dad enter the kitchen. Mom began giving him the lowdown immediately. I could not hear his reply. I broke out in a sweat as I continued to wait. Nothing, not a footstep. Was I reprieved? Not a chance. Then his tread on the stairs. Instantly, my brothers scattered to other bedrooms. It seemed to take an eternity for Dad to mount the stairs. "Please, God, let me disappear!"

Finally, he was there, at the door to my bedroom, and yes, he was giving me The Look. It shot through me like a laser beam. I felt eradicated—nebulized! Then the third degree began: "Do you have any idea what could have happened to you and Billy out there? Huh? Do you?"

It was not a rhetorical question. I had to come up with a reply, and a good one.

"I could have sprained my ankle," I offered.

"If you were lucky!" Dad shot back. "Come on, what could have happened to you?"

I had to say it—that I could have been hit by a train—and, of course, saying those words started the tears coming. But that did not stop the third degree from continuing.

"What would you have done if Billy had gotten his foot caught in the tracks?"

Years later, I would realize that this line of questioning was part of Dad's reflexive lesson-giving—preparing me for the unexpected out there on the perimeter. But at that moment, at the age of seven, all I knew was that I had to keep coming up with acceptable answers. It went on for probably ten minutes and then Dad shifted into punishment mode. My brothers had been right: one month in the yard, no parade. It was almost a relief; at least the worst part—incurring Dad's wrath—was over. Needless to say, I did not venture to the railroad tracks again.

Flash forward. It is a spring Saturday last year and I am doing the lawn. My two older sons, Colin and Ian, have gone out biking. The house rule is that they cannot go farther than three blocks. My wife, Elena, is inside, catching up on some paperwork for her job. I don't hear it, but the phone rings, and suddenly Elena is signaling me to stop the mower. It was the police. Ian ran into a ditch and his bike is broken. He is fine, except for a few scrapes and scratches. They have to be picked up. They are in Stockbridge—*five miles from home*!

The rest of the scenario plays out as if we have rehearsed it a thousand times—and indeed we have. Elena goes in the van to pick up the boys, while I continue mowing. I know that she will say nary a word to them when she finds them, that the three of them will ride back home in stony silence. When they arrive, I do not look up from my lawn work, but in my peripheral vision see them march despondently inside. I let them wait up in their room for a good fifteen minutes before I turn off the mower and go inside—I know how crucial that period of anxious waiting is in disciplining my boys. It gives them time not only to worry about what I will do but also to prepare themselves for the inevitable questions I will grill them with. I slowly wash up, and then enter their room. I can feel The Look already forming on my face. To tell the absolute truth, there is a part of me that finds The Look and my role in all of this slightly comical; I am more self-conscious about it than my father ever was, and hence I can see the edge of absurdity in my repeating this time-honored role. What's more, I know that my savvy eldest son, Ian, will detect this sense of absurdity in me and will play to it, trying to get out of trouble by making me an ally, a fellow see-througher of this charade. But I will not give in to him. I cannot. He has to learn what is acceptable behavior and what is not, especially out there on the perimeter, and it is my duty as his father to make sure that he does. I give The Look, I administer the third degree, I lay out the punishment (two weeks of no biking).

I have done my job and Elena has done hers. I may have done mine with more self-consciousness and less severity than my own father did, but I have essentially played the same fathering role. And whatever else one may say about this, *it seems to work*. My boys, in general, are learning the rules and obeying them. And I am convinced that they are assimilating this guide to behavior better by the way Elena and I are delivering it to them than if I, in the name of being a more momlike parent, curtailed my aggressive, confrontational impulse and inhibited The Look.

I cannot tell you how many New Involved Fathers I have seen who have been made to feel uncomfortable with their disciplinary instincts. Instead of showing their anger and throwing The Look, they say things to the rule-breaking child like, "Let's try to understand why you did this wrong thing, Joey," and my absolute least favorite, "You don't know how much it hurts me when you behave like that, Joey" (all guilt and no guidance). If *both* parents approach discipline in this feminized manner, the outcome is likely to be a spoiled, somewhat neurotic child.

One couple, Mark and Kristen, came to see me because their kindergartner, Tim, was driving his teacher up the wall: whenever this teacher gave the boy instructions to do something or to stop doing something, he responded with, "Why?" or "Why are you asking me to do this?" or "Am I doing this for me or for you?" Truly precocious questions, but certainly maddening ones that were making this little guy into a much-too-powerful little brat. Had they done something wrong in bringing up their son? These parents wanted to know.

"It looks like your son thinks everyone is going to be as

tolerant of his quiz game as apparently both of you are," I replied.

It was a fairly obvious observation, but it apparently struck Mark like a thunderbolt. He said that he and Kristen had agreed early on to give their son every opportunity to question them about anything that puzzled him—in fact, they had agreed to encourage this because Kristen wanted him to understand things, rather than just be "an automaton who does what he is told to do." And so, following Kristen's lead, Mark had adopted the endlessly patient tone with their son that she employed.

"You mean, that tone doesn't really come naturally to you?" I ventured.

"Well, not really," Mark replied. I noticed that his wife seemed surprised and somewhat disappointed by his answer.

"So when Tim asks you for the third time why he should wear his jacket, what would your instincts have you do, rather than patiently try to answer his question?" I asked.

"Do what my dad did, I guess," he said.

What his dad did turned out to be to give The Look.

"And you don't give Tim The Look because you think it's too cruel?"

"My father was not a very warm or forgiving man," was Mark's answer.

"I think you can give your son The Look when the occasion demands it and still be a warm and forgiving father to him," I said. "Why don't you give it a try and see if Tim shapes up at school?"

Kristen glared at me. "Well, I'm not going to stop being a patient mother with him!" she declared.

"I don't think you'll need to," I told her. "My guess is that The Look will be enough for both of you."

As it turned out, my advice worked, and rather quickly. And, with a mother who still indulged his persistence, Tim seemed none the worse for it.

One reason that today's Involved Dad has been induced to back away from his fathering instincts when it comes to disciplining his children is because these instincts have become associated with abuse. I have actually heard one well-meaning psychologist declare that under certain circumstances, "looking cross-eyed" at your child amounts to "emotional abuse." And so once again Dad is so fraught with *guilt* (associated with being a potential abuser) and so *confused* (by what his appropriate role as disciplinarian should be) that he withdraws from the whole scene. Rather than be a "bad" father, he opts to be no father at all.

We have become so sensitized to our child's precarious emotional makeup and to his or her fragile sense of self-esteem that we have become terrified of ever showing our disapproval—*even when our child misbehaves*. In my opinion, this too-ginger treatment of our kids has actually *contributed* to their emotional fragility. If they never experience our disapproval in the form of The Look and The Severe Talking-to and The Punishment, they tend to become such delicate, precious creatures that they are totally unprepared for the rules and disapproval out there in the world. Yes, our children need our unconditional love, but they also need our guidance on how to behave in the world.

We cannot leave the topic of discipline and abuse without touching on the sensitive subject of corporal punishment. Spankings and the "back of the hand" are clearly more traditionally associated with fathers than with mothers. So, unfortunately, are severe beatings with belts and whips. There are many people who see no distinction between a spanking and a whipping—both are considered damaging physical abuse. Personally, I was raised with very little corporal punishment and, in turn, I have brought up my children that way; I find that The Look smarts more than any spanking. But nonetheless, I think it is extremely dangerous not to make a distinction between a spanking and a whipping, *to see abuse everywhere*. This blurring of distinctions can trickle down in a way that makes us totally impotent as disciplinarians, turning us into fathers who are so inhibited by the specter of being an "abuser" that we dare not aggressively demonstrate to our children the difference between acceptable and unacceptable behavior.

It is interesting to note here that today in our country most *real and cruel* physical abuse is perpetrated on children by mothers and by men in the home who are not the children's biological fathers. Obviously, the primary reason this is true is because so many abandoned mothers are left with the task of being both mother and father to their children. This surprising fact should not be taken as an apology or alibi for any child abuse, whether perpetrated by dads, moms, or anyone else. But it does comprise one more significant reason why it is important for fathers to be in the home and to be involved in their children's upbringing. Yet, paradoxically, some of us have taken the very real problem of child abuse and used it as an argument *against* traditional confrontational (albeit compassionate) fathering.

In the last analysis, fathers perform the function of disciplining their children first and foremost simply by *being there*. A father who is not present on a continuing basis, through the good times and the bad, can never hope to be an effective disciplinary force. If he simply makes a special (and rare) appearance to read his kid the riot act, he may instill fear in his child, but not respect, and the outcome is more likely to be an angry, rebellious child than a well-adjusted and well-behaved one. But the Involved Dad with a consistent presence in his child's life will garner his child's respect even as he throws The Look, gives The Talking-to, and lays out The Punishment. His child knows that Dad is more than just the heavy; he is the man who can teach him how to deal with the limits out there in the world.

"Be a Team Player, but Stake Out Your Territory!"/ "Be Yourself and the Rest Will Take Care of Itself."

A few weekends ago, I drove down to have dinner with my parents. I am, I like to think, a grown man: I am in my forties, I have a thriving professional practice, I am married and have three children. Yet there is nothing like taking my place at my parents' dinner table for me to feel like I am eighteen years old and for my parents to behave accordingly. (In fact, of the eight now-vacant seats at the table, I still take the same one that I did growing up.)

The meal started off well with a discussion of my boys, in these quarters known as *their grandchildren*. Then we moved on to current national politics. But at around this point, I observed that my mother had more or less dropped out of the conversation and was gazing intently at my face, in particular at my beard and longish hair. Finally, she could not hold it back any longer.

"When are you going to cut it?" she asked, as Dad and I addressed the pros and cons of welfare reform.

That was all my father needed to launch into the real political issue that was on his mind.

"You know what I can't figure out, Johnny?" he said. "Is your hair too long because you are underemployed, or are you underemployed because your hair is too long?" (My father, who throughout his life had been a hardworking employee, finds it hard to make the distinction between "underemployed" and "self-employed.")

Once I remembered that I really was not eighteen years old, I had to smile: Mom and Dad were playing out their time-honored roles. When my mother looked at my long hair, she reflexively thought that something must be going badly in her son's life for him to be "letting himself go" like this; she was worried about my inner life. My father, on the other hand, looked at my locks and reflexively wanted to know how my hair length was affecting my place in the professional world; he was concerned about my social and economic standing.

All is well, I thought to myself. My mom and dad are still working in tandem to help their little boy become well balanced, both emotionally secure and competitive. I suppose I still need all the help I can get.

I see these dad/mom antimonies successfully playing out in families all the time. Dad wants to know if his daughter is popular at school, if she gets along well with the other kids, if she has staked out her area of excellence. He may not ask her leading questions about these topics, but he is tuned in to them; the lessons he teaches her by either example or tutorial are aimed at guiding her to become more successful in these areas. Mom, on the other hand, is more interested in knowing if her daughter is happy at school, if she feels fulfilled there; and in the social realm, she is more concerned about whether her daughter has a good friend than if she is popular.

Once again, I say Dad and Mom are a good combo. From Dad, daughter learns the harsh realities of the pecking order, the ins and outs of membership, teamwork, and leadership. From Mom, daughter learns the importance of individuality and personal satisfaction.

Last winter I brought my son Ian home from a soccer game that his team had lost pretty badly. He walked into our house dejected. Throwing his gym bag down, he groaned, "We should've won!"

Immediately, my wife came in from her office, looked at him sympathetically, and said, "How do you feel about how *you* played, Ian?"

Before he could answer that one, I blurted out what I thought was the real problem at the game I had just witnessed: "They could have won if they'd played better as a team. Too much dribbling and not enough passing."

Elena's and my responses came straight out of the Dad/Mom Playbook. Ian got the emotional hug he needed from Mom, the lowdown on teamwork from a dad who heartily approved of trying to win. Later on that evening, Ian knocked on my study door; he wanted to know how I thought the team could play better as a group. I suggested that he could take on some leadership in that area by *only* passing during the next few games and see if it caught on with the others. (It did.)

To be sure, a father's concern with his child's social standing can go out of kilter if left unchecked—that is to say, without the countervailing influence of the child's mother. I saw this extreme more than once during the Vietnam War. When one friend of mine declared that he would flee to Canada if his draft lottery number was picked, his father howled, "And shame the family?"

My friend was devastated. "Would you rather I came home in a box than bring shame on this house?" he screamed back.

Fortunately, at that moment his mother intervened. She embraced her son and Dad backed away.

The moral question here was tricky, as it was for many families in my hometown at that time. But inasmuch as my friend's father was more concerned with his boy's (and his family's) social standing than with his personal honor and duty, I am very glad that his mom was there to invoke her maternal concern of love above all.

"Goodbye and Good Luck, Pal!" / "We're Always Here for You, Sweetie!"

A friend of mine who was getting married for the first time rather late in life was dithering out loud about whether or not he should have children. Every man he had talked to had said that having a kid was the best thing that ever happened to him, but still my friend was unsure; he felt that none of his friends was being honest with him about the downside of having a child.

"Okay, you want the *real* downside?" I said. "The whole thing is a diabolical setup! You are presented with this little thing and you know instantly that you are going to love this thing more than anybody or anything in your entire life. Then you are handed the book of instructions that comes with this little thing and the first rule in that book is, 'Your job is to make this little person totally independent of you.' In other words, your job from Day One is to teach your child how to leave you behind. Now *that's* diabolical!"

This particular job is one that dads—no matter how heart-breaking it can be for them—are best prepared to perform. From the get-go, Dad is the parent who is most likely to support and promote autonomy, the move toward the perimeter; Dad is the parent who most takes to heart the admonition that our pediatrician gave to Elena and me at the end of our first checkup for our firstborn son. "Remember," the doctor said, "you only have him on loan."

If Dad achieves the goal of teaching total autonomy just in time for his child to leave the nest, he can feel a sense of accomplishment (one that *almost* makes up for his feeling of loss). Here, probably more than in any other part of life, the child needs to feel the power of both parental lessons/messages: Dad's, which says, "I have prepared you well to get along out there without us"; and Mom's, which says, "Wherever you go and whatever you do, you will always have our support."

But if Dad becomes more momlike and holds on to his child as much as moms are wont to do, he will be doing both his child and himself a disservice.

I remember in college there were some boys who every week sent their laundry home in cardboard-and-strap packages for Mom to do. I found the whole procedure baffling and slightly comical. (Of course, I came from a family of eight children; my mother was mightily relieved to have one less load to wash.) Finally, I asked one of these boys if he didn't think it would be cheaper and easier to do his own laundry at the Laundromat.

"Sure," he replied. "But it would break my mother's heart!"

But not his father's, I bet.

✻   ✻   ✻

Let me bring this chapter to a close on a controversial note.

One significant way that parents move their children along toward adult independence is by helping them to define and accept their sexuality. Here, the relative tendencies of dads and moms often come into conflict, especially in this era of hypersensitivity to issues of appropriate sexual behavior and respect, not to mention the increased sex-associated health risks.

Last summer, friends of mine who are parents of a sixteen-year-old son related just such a conflict to me. Their son had met an older, college girl at his summer job whom he found attractive; happily, the young woman found him attractive too and they started to go out together after work. But Mom was worried; she thought the girl was too old for her son, that she might be too "fast" for him, and that she might break his heart. Mom kept admonishing her son that he was going to regret this relationship. Dad, on the other hand, thought the idea of his son having a summer romance was terrific; he believed he was ready for one both emotionally and in terms of personal responsibility, that it was natural, and that it would make him happy. He told his wife that he thought she was a killjoy. "Let the boy have some fun," he said. "He doesn't have to marry the girl."

Fortunately, this was an open family in which the son heard both of his parents' unfiltered points of view. And hearing both points of view, this young man did what any well-balanced offspring would do—he acted on both of them: he had his summer romance with the college girl, but he did so cautiously, not giving away his heart too quickly or too easily. If that is not a healthy step toward responsible and happy adult sexuality, I do not know what is.

Obviously, if their child had been a girl, the above scenario might have played out differently: moms can often be more romantic-minded when it comes to their daughters than dads; and, of course, some dads see all boys as unworthy of their daughters. But in general, contemporary Involved Dads are still more likely than moms to urge both their sons and their daughters to press ahead in the gradual development of their sexual selves.

Dads, for example, are prone to say to their developing daughters, "You're getting so beautiful, darling."

This fatherly observation can go a long way to make his daughter comfortable with her sexual development and attractiveness. Yet today there are legions of people who consider themselves "psychologically aware" who would find Dad's compliment "inappropriate behavior," too seductive—in fact, bordering on sexual abuse.

"Baloney!" I say. A dad who spontaneously compliments his daughter's appearance is behaving absolutely appropriately. Delivered with warmth and pride, his approval will contribute to her healthy sexual development. And when a dad does this, it goes further in this cause than any compliment from a mom.

If you are wondering just how far I intend to take this line of thought, stay tuned. There was a time when fathers out on a walk with their teenage sons would gaze appreciatively at an attractive woman passing by in, say, a halter top and short-shorts. These fathers might even have verbalized their admiration with (dare I say it?), "Wow, look at the legs on her!" But now that we have been told that such an observation is sexist and demeaning to women, we have learned to desist from such gazes and comments, *especially* in front of our sons, because we are shaping the way our boys perceive, value, and think about women.

But hold the phone for a moment. What lesson are we giving our maturing sons when we *do not react at all* to a passing beauty? Are we not conveying to them that sexual attractiveness is of no real importance, that at the very least it should be ignored? This is not the message I want to send to my boys when they reach puberty, among other reasons because it will not jibe with the sexual feelings that they are experiencing and will only serve to further distance them from me at a time when it is important for us to keep in good contact with one another.

I am not saying that we should be openly crude and salacious in the presence of our pubescent sons. Furthermore, we should establish a model of respectful behavior. We never say, "Look at the legs on her!" within earshot of the woman. No whistling or catcalls either. And in deference to the boy's mother, I would counsel against such appreciative gazes and comments in front of her or any other woman companion. Also, it is important that we share *all* our observations about the opposite sex with our boys, including, "Wow, is she smart!" and "Look at the powerful serve she's got!" But I also want my son to know that appreciating feminine pulchritude is not only natural, but one of the great pleasures of a man's life. For me to ignore those fine-looking legs on that beauty passing by us would be to do my son a serious disservice in preparing him for manhood.

My point is simple but, I believe, far-reaching: in the name of gender parity, let us not contribute to the desexualization of our culture. Just as, in the name of parent parity, we should not contribute to androgenous fathering and mothering. A dad is not a mom, and that turns out to be good news for everyone concerned.

5

The Working Father's Burden

▼ ▼ ▼ ▼

The "Paternity-Leave-Is-for-Girls" Syndrome (and Other On-the-Job Self-Defeating Mind-sets)

If the mind-sets and stereotypes that block our way to becoming Marathon Dads at *home* seem formidable, those that block our way in the *workplace* are positively stupendous. In our culture, the mythology of what it is to be a "real man" permeates virtually every thought we have about ourselves and what we as men ought to do—and nowhere is this as pervasive as in our work culture. These myths routinely prevent us from making decisions and changing behavior that could make our lives as productive workers *and* hands-on fathers incredibly easier and more fulfilling.

These are the facts: as many working fathers as working mothers say that they experience serious conflicts between reconciling the demands of work with the demands of parenthood, *yet only two percent of the men who are eligible for paternity leave from their jobs actually take it.* Similarly, relative to working mothers, only a very small percentage of working fathers take advantage of family-friendly company policies that allow sick-child leave, flexible work schedules, or working-from-home arrangements.

So it appears that it is not simply corporate policy that is keeping us from making radical changes in the way we parcel

out our time between work and home; it is something else—
something in our heads that we seem to be having a real
problem shaking loose. Now, I am in no way suggesting that
every eligible father should take advantage of paternity leave
or sick-child leave or flex time or working-from-home deals,
but I am very strongly urging all of us to be conscious and
clear about why *we do* or *do not* take advantage of these
policies. And if it turns out that what is preventing us from
even considering these policies is some myth or stereotype
that we have uncritically accepted or some fear that is revealed
to be unfounded, then we owe it to ourselves to cut the crap
and clear our heads. After that, perhaps we will want to take
a second look at these opportunities to see if they might actually be helpful in making our lives as Marathon Dads easier,
less stressful, and more productive.

Most of the stereotypes, mind-sets, and fears that we delve
into here have implications that go far beyond the question of
whether or not we take advantage of family-friendly company
policies; they affect our behavior and choices in virtually every
arena where we try to reconcile our professional lives with
our fathering/husbanding lives. But I find something especially
instructive in looking at these mind-sets from the perspective
of our typically male responses to family-friendly company policies: it has the clarity of a cardinal case, and it sets up a sharp
contrast between the "head" problems of working fathers and
those of working mothers.

One last thought before we move on: the great majority of
us who want to be successful Marathon Dads do *not* go around
saying (or even seriously thinking) things like, "If God had
wanted us to take care of babies, He would have given us
breasts." On the contrary, we sincerely want to leave such old
prejudices behind so we can get on with reconciling our family
lives with our professional lives. But the male mind is a cun-
ning thing: we seem to know intuitively how to take our old,
outdated prejudices and give them a spin that makes them
unrecognizable—even to ourselves. And so we often find our-

selves talking the talk of New Fatherhood without walking the walk. In the chapters that follow, we will try to do a little unspinning of these disguised myths and prejudices.

The Wimp Factor

I need to start with a confession. Remember that quintessential Marathon Dad I described at the outset—the guy with the pacifier peeking over the top of his breast pocket? Well, several years ago, when I was just beginning to wrestle with the problems of sharing the home workload with my working wife, I happened to glimpse my first pacifier-packing pop in a bank queue and I had the following fleeting thought: *Geez, next thing you know, this guy will be growing a pair to go with that plastic nipple!*

It was only a flash before I caught myself. And heaven knows I am not proud of my piggy reflex, brief though it was. But it did alert me to the tenacity of my habitual male prejudices. At that moment I realized that becoming a Marathon Dad was going to involve a hell of a lot more than simply working out new ways of scheduling my time; it was going to involve keeping a close eye on myself for die-hard responses that could all too easily sabotage my intentions of working out ways to reconcile my work life with my family life.

I am not talking about setting up some kind of internal Thought Police here—all that could come of something like that is more guilt and confusion. What I am talking about is *consciousness.* If every time I see a man with a pacifier in his pocket or a man toting an infant in a Snugly, and I reflexively think, *"Wimp!"* then I had better be aware of that reflex and where it comes from. Because if I am not conscious of it, it is going to influence the choices I make in tricky, self-defeating ways.

Speaking with men, both in a therapy setting and casually, I have discovered that most of us are deeply wimp-conscious. Our philosophies may be liberated, but we carry within us a terror of wimpdom—of being perceived by others as a wimp, or worse, perceiving ourselves as one. A wimp is a man without backbone, a pushover, a "good boy" who does what he is told. (In a German sociology book I read, "wimp" was translated as a "wet dishrag.") He is a man who collapses under pressure, especially if that pressure comes in the form of a scolding, displeased woman. In the last analysis, there is something distinctly feminine about a wimp (one of my friends believes that the term derives from "**w**oman **imp**oster"). Therefore, whatever male behavior we perceive as being feminized elicits the Wimp! response. Naturally, much of this so-called feminized behavior is simply men doing what used to be called women's work. And there, of course, is the rub.

Wimps' Portraits Don't Hang on the Boardroom Wall

Every company has its own historical legacy, its own enduring legends about the heroes who founded the establishment or who brought it back from the brink and made it the profitable place it is today. You can see oil portraits of these people on the boardroom wall; they are our corporate royalty. Well, one thing is immediately apparent about these heroes—they are all guys. And chances are they did not end up with their portraits on the wall by taking paternity leave.

So what we have here is a culture whose heroes stand foursquare on the side of giving one's heart and soul (not to mention 100 hours a week) to his job. Not to put too fine a point on it, but it is obviously going to take more than a few enlightened company policies to reform the culture of the place so much that the guy who takes advantage of these policies finds his portrait hanging side by side with those of the old-line heroes. And that is just for starters.

Girl Policies vs. Boy Policies

One rationale that men give for not taking advantage of their employer's family-friendly policies is that these policies were created for working mothers, not working fathers. The only reason these policies are also offered to men (the rationale continues) is to give them the *appearance* of gender neutrality. This makes them legally nondiscriminatory; and what is more, women like company policies to be gender-neutral because then they can feel more "equal" in the workplace. But the truth is (the rationale concludes), no one really expects *a man*—and certainly not the *majority* of men—to take paternity leave.

Whether it is explicit or not, the thought lurking behind all of this is, *Only a wimp would take advantage of girl policies*. Part of our wimp reaction comes from a low-level confusion: because working mothers were the first to create the need for family-friendly policies like maternity leave, and because working mothers supplied the leadership and political clout to put these policies in place, we assume the policies themselves are somehow feminine. Not necessarily so. Yes, we have working mothers to *thank* for these policies, but perhaps we should literally thank them because, as working fathers, we have many of the same time needs and time binds that working mothers had before us.

One reason this is so hard for us to swallow is because in the past decade we have grown wary of the feminization of the workplace, at times for legitimate reasons. Indeed, some of the changes brought about by the large influx of women to the workplace may *not* be good for us; they run contrary to a work ethic that has served us well. I am thinking, for example, of risk-taking; this is a quality that professional men generally prize and have historically reaped benefits from, yet which fewer professional women feel comfortable with and so weigh in against at company meetings. But the jump from resisting this particular "feminization" of the workplace to resisting *all* ideas, practices, and policies introduced by women is a mistaken one. It is, in fact, the mistake inherent to most prejudices: mistaking the particular for the general. We should judge the value of each of these policies by how well it suits our personal needs and desires as working fathers, unclouded by any confusions.

Before we move on to other variations on the Wimp Factor, we need to acknowledge one particular group of people in the workplace who may very well be sending us messages that say, in effect, *"Hey, pal, don't really use these family policies— not if you are a real company guy."* I am speaking, of course, of our employers. When such employers discuss their brand-new family-friendly policies with other men, it is accompanied by the smiles, winks, and nods that tell the genuine story: *"Don't touch it, pal!"* All we have to do is recall the reported winks and nods that accompanied talk of affirmative action in the hallowed halls of Texaco to know what is going on here. Subtle or unsubtle, the message is clear: *"You would be a wimp if you actually took paternity leave—and your career would seriously suffer for it."* Later on, when I discuss the fears we have which prevent us from taking advantage of various family policies, I will lay out some techniques for sorting rational workplace fears from paranoid ones. I will also look into what our options are when those fears really are well founded, as in the above winks-and-nods scenario. But for now, let us stay with how the Wimp Factor as an *irrational* mind-set prevents us from taking advantage of "girl" policies and radically limits our options.

"Hey, We All Know This Is Just a Passing Phase"

Here's a myth that lingers somewhere in the preconscious of many men: at rock bottom, we persist in believing that this business of working women is just a temporary aberration, a blip on the screen that will soon disappear and then everything will go back to "normal" again. I am not suggesting that this is a turn of events we *actively* hope will happen, just one that seems likely in our befuddled minds. The rest of this goofy assumption goes something like this: *"This working-women thing is going to turn out to be just like Nehru jackets and* *bell-bottoms, artifacts of a forgotten era. So why should we make any adjustments when we are just going to have to change back again when all this passes? Hey, when the Old Order returns, it's the guys with the foresight **not** to take paternity leave or flex time who will be on top."*

This, of course, is simply one of our old-time male prejudices dressed up as "mature farsightedness." In fact, all the evidence out there points to the fact that women in the workplace are here to stay—at the very least for the duration of our working lives. So let's weed out this counterproductive myth before it irrationally influences any of our decisions.

On Trying to Look Debonair with a Pacifier in Your Pocket

One of the predictable effects of The Great Migration of women into the workplace is the eroticization of the office. As the number of women and men on the job reach parity and as gender contact there increases, sexual attraction and all the behavior that follows from it explode. Some of that behavior can, of course, be terribly destructive to families, but it is not my intention here to get into the fallout of office love affairs. What is relevant here is the increased importance we men attach to our sexual attractiveness in the workplace; being attractive there and the feedback that attractiveness garners us in the form of approving sidelong glances, office flirtations and romances, along with what one of my friends calls "that ever-present tingle," have become two of the perks of going to work. According to Arlie Hochschild, this sexual frisson at the office is one reason many people of both sexes prefer spending time there to spending it at home—by contrast, a house full of kids, laundry, and other demands is not very sexy at all.

But neither is a man at the office with a pacifier in his pocket.

Let's face it, few women are going to find him a turn-on—

especially not women who consider the workplace a sanctuary from home and all reminders thereof. Yup, it's the old Wimp Factor again. And this time it hits us where it hurts the most: in our male sexuality. By extension, taking paternity leave or flex time can have the same effect as carrying a pacifier in our breast pocket. Both men and women may have come a long way philosophically, *but a man doing what used to be called women's work remains seriously unsexy, particularly to the women at work.*

The irony here is unmistakable: the liberated women with whom we share our home lives encourage us to pitch in and do our share of home duties, while the liberated women with whom we share our professional lives encourage us (no doubt unwittingly) to be "sexy," that is, pacifier-forsaking, paternity-leave-renouncing *real men.* Talk about trying to please two exacting mistresses!

What's a man to do—especially a sexually vain man, if that's not a redundancy? Many of us feel that we have already all but abandoned our sexy image at home; do we now have to give up our last shred of sexual pride in the one place it still flourishes?

Well, one solution is to stop carrying pacifiers in our pockets. I am serious. If it is basically appearances that we are talking about here, let us address the problem where it lives—in our *style* of being Marathon Dads. Whenever I spend time at a vacation home in a small village in Greece, I am struck by how common it is to see Greek men tote their babies and youngsters along the paths and harbor lines—and how they do so in a decidedly masculine way. They carry them on their shoulders, sling them under their arms like squealing pigs, balance a pair of them in their arms like so many sacks of grain—they do it casually, perhaps a bit roughly by maternal standards, but they clearly do it with pride and affection. And, as my wife will attest, they look damned sexy doing so. Perhaps this Greek male method of baby-toting is less convenient and less efficient than using a Snugli, but I believe it is ultimately more comfortable than a Snugli would be for these men, and, by extension, for most men. The task is being done without sacrificing one's personal masculine style of doing things or one's sex appeal. Here, then, is another facet of the Daddy-Is-Not-a-Mommy phenomenon: there is no reason we need to do our parenting tasks *stylistically* in a mommylike way or in a mommy-approved way. In fact, when we do such tasks our own way, they usually cease to look like "women's work," and that can make doing them a whole lot easier on our psyches.

But can there be a sexy, masculine style to taking paternity leave or flex time or sick-child leave? I believe so. I can envision a liberated, masculine father on a paternity leave that includes golf games with the baby bouncing on top of the golf bag between holes; I can imagine him leaving his office at three o'clock in the afternoon on a motorcycle to pick up his kid at school. And this guy does not strike me as a wimp— nor, I believe, does he strike his female co-workers that way, those women who are wistfully watching him mount his motorcycle through the office window. On the contrary, gentlemen.

Our Own Dads Didn't, Wouldn't, Won't

Clearly, the basic way we learned how to be fathers was from our own fathers—we watched them and absorbed their attitudes and styles. But by and large, our dads did their dad thing in a time when few mothers worked and few fathers helped out around the house. So, in general, thinking and acting like our own dads does not put us on the road to becoming a successful Marathon Dad.

This is hardly news to most of us. One of the chief reasons people have trouble changing their mind-sets and behavior about *anything* is an absence of models to guide or inspire these changes. But what compounds the problem for us is that often our fathers (and mothers and in-laws) *actively deter us from straying from the model of fatherhood that they have lived by.* Dad wants us to be like him and he not only says so, he occasionally utters (or at least implies) the Wimp Word if we perform what in his day was solely women's work. This is a more prevalent phenomenon than many people imagine. I cannot begin to tell you how many men have reported to me incidents where their father or mother, father-in-law or mother-in-law, has come out and said words to the effect of "You should be ashamed of yourself for making your wife (my daughter) take a job," or "Paternity leave? Isn't that for breast-feeding women?"

And even though I explain to these men that their parents are simply protecting their own traditional turf, that they are afraid a new way of doing things will invalidate the way they have already done things, their words sting. As any card-carrying psychologist will tell you, parental disapproval has untold power, even when we are grown men with good jobs and fabulous backhands. The result is one more piece of Wimp Factor resistance to taking paternity leave or sick-child leave or working-at-home options—or a raft of other changes, for that matter.

Money and Manhood

A sex therapist I know says that he can estimate the number of new cases of psychologically based impotence he will see by looking at the financial page. "As the Dow Jones goes down, so do erections," he quips. I offer his observation as an example of just how closely money—in particular, earning power—is tied to our sense of manhood. So when I say that many men resist considering flex-time or part-time work as an option simply because the money stinks, we understand that this is not simply cold economics that is involved, it is also a variation on the Wimp Factor, as in *"Only a wimp would willingly choose the lesser-paying job."*

Interestingly, in Sweden, where men on paternity leave receive 100 percent of their normal pay for eight months, the great majority of men take advantage of this option—even male immigrants from super-macho cultures like Turkey and Morocco. Which leads me to believe that if the money is right, our self-image can make the adjustment. We should hold on to this thought for later, when we consider the political options of Marathon Dad.

The money-and-manhood phenomenon comes into play when men give the following reason for not taking advantage of family-friendly policies: *"I need to give an honest day's work for an honest day's pay. That's the working man's credo—something that working women do not completely understand."* Never mind that some men who talk this way think nothing of routinely putting in only four hours of productive work in an eight-hour day (that is, after all the time chatting around the water cooler, grabbing a coffee, phoning friends, and playing computer games is subtracted).

A variation on the "honest day's work" line is, *"Paternity leave is just a form of welfare, and real men don't feed at the welfare trough."* Many men consciously hold on to this point of view in spite of growing statistics which show that most family-friendly policies increase productivity and profits for the company; in other words, as far as the company is concerned, these policies actually represent enlightened self-interest. But our main concern here is those of us who *unconsciously* hang on to this way of thinking and allow it to influence—and possibly sabotage—our options. Again, check yourself out.

A further variation on this theme goes like this: *"These are my peak moneymaking years, so I've got to make hay while the sun shines—I can't possibly take paternity leave now."* Of course, the implication of this kind of thinking is that the best time to take paternity leave is when we're too old to have children. But even putting that aside, there remains plenty of room for self-deceit, because in the last analysis, we tend to think of *every* working year as potentially our best moneymaking year.

Perhaps the most insidious form of money/manhood think-ing is the one that goes like this: *"Hey, I believe in equality as much as anybody—but the bottom line has to be* financial *equality, right?"* From this thought it is just a hop, skip, and jump to *"Look, I happen to earn one and a half times what my wife earns, so when it comes down to deciding who's going to be where when, money's got to figure into the equation, right? In other words, if my time at work is more financially valuable to the family than my wife's time at work, that means it makes more sense for my wife to take time off from her job to take care of the baby than for me to take time off from mine."*

Obviously, dollars and cents *do* have to figure in such deci-sions, but, once again, money has a way of taking on a sym-bolic life of its own for many men. We may actually find ourselves believing that if we get paid more at our job than our wife gets paid at hers, our time is *in general* more valuable than hers. From that, it is all too easy to rationalize lying on the couch at the end of the workday while the wife makes dinner and bathes the kids at the end of hers: *"Hey, I earned more money, so it all equals out!"* Never mind that we have worked *equally* hard for an *equal* number of hours and are *equally* tired.

But I do not want to get into any feminist-type sermons here; there are loads of women out there to take on that job. Again, all I want to do is keep our heads clear of unreason—especially unreason that backs us into corners of guilt and recrimination and phony excuses that eventually come back to haunt and confuse us.

Team Play Is a Guy Thing

This one begins in the gym culture of junior high and high school and lingers in the male consciousness through all of our lives: it is the ethic of the team player and it is definitely part of being a "real man." A team player never abandons his teammates and never leaves the game until it is over—certainly not just because Mommy calls him home (only a wimp would do that). And so a team player in the professional world cannot let his mates down by taking paternity leave or sick-child leave or work-at-home options—certainly not because his wife says she needs his help at home. It is simply not the honorable thing to do, and the reason women do not understand and accept that is because team play is a guy thing.

But let's look at a few semicomfortable facts surrounding this "honorable thing." First, team play turns out to be as much of a *girl thing* if not more so. For example, studies show that professional women in general have more highly developed cooperation and communication skills when it comes to accomplishing a group task than men do. And second, let's be consistent here: taking care of the children *also* requires team play—on that basic team composed of you and your wife. So all the team-play argument really comes down to is that perennial conflict of Marathon Dad: *how can I be loyal to two teams at the same time?* We all know that the answer to that question is complicated; and at the very least, we know that it cannot be resolved by simply claiming to be a team player.

It's a Bird! It's a Plane! It's Super Dad!

We seek our last refuge from wimpdom by flying to the other extreme, by insisting that we are perfectly capable of doing it all—job and fathering—without any special help or considerations. We look back on the short-lived Super Mom phenomenon that was in vogue when women first started entering the workforce in large numbers and think, *Sure, the reason that didn't last is because women don't have what it takes to do it all. But I do. I'm a guy and I don't need any extra help. Super Dad doesn't feed at the company welfare trough.*

This attitude does not need a detailed rebuttal from me or anyone else. Simply trying to do it all—*really* do it all—for a few months should be enough to cure any honest man of this delusion. The fact is, if we are genuinely going to perform both of our jobs well, we need all the help we can get, whether that help is in the form of taking advantage of a company family policy or "outsourcing" some of our family duties or radically restructuring our schedules—or all three. And anybody who does not believe that has a serious Wimp Factor problem.

6

Hidden Hurdles at Home

▼ ▼ ▼ ▼

Guy Guilt

Of all the characteristics that working mothers seem to want to own exclusively, the one that baffles me the most is "guilt." I cannot pick up a book or magazine article about so-called Super Moms without the G word popping up, often along with some snide aside to the effect that guilt is something that working fathers do not have to deal with.

Well, I am a therapist whose practice consists largely of working fathers, and believe me, we are hardly strangers to guilt. It is not my intention here to participate in a round of "Guiltier Than Thou" with working moms, but I do need to set the record straight by saying that we working fathers experience our fair share of guilt and we somehow manage to do so without having to "get in touch with our feminine side." The unhappy fact is that we do feel guilty a great deal of the time, guilty that we are not doing our jobs as well as we should as a result of family demands, guilty that we are not being good enough husbands and fathers as a result of work demands, and guilty that we are failing to fulfill ourselves as a result of both.

Guilt is hardly something to be proud of. It is bad for our health and our performance, reducing our effectiveness as both worker and father and taking the joy out of both spheres in the bargain. And then, to make matters even worse, it goes on to infect the people around us.

Bad-Daddy Guilt

Above all, we are guilty as fathers. We are guilty for missing Little League games and dance recitals, for not helping with homework, for not showing up for dinner, for not playing a game of catch after dinner—in short, guilty for simply not being there for our children enough of the time. Ancillary to this guilt is the nagging feeling that we are not providing our children with enough of the fatherly, male-figure lessons and modeling that we are uniquely capable of contributing.

But before we get into how this guilt, if unexamined, can make us even more deficient at fathering, I should note that "Bad-Daddy Guilt" often does serve a very important function: *it signals us that we may actually be behaving badly.* After all, we really *should* be trying to make it to those Little League games and dance recitals; we really *should* be helping with homework, showing up for dinner, and playing catch afterward at least some of the time—and probably more of the time than we are now. Much of this book, particularly Part II, will offer some concrete methods for time management that will enable us to be there as fathers more of the time. But even then, Bad-Daddy Guilt may not abate entirely—guilt is clingy stuff. And so it is doubly important for us to understand how this guilt plays out in our lives and how it affects our children.

Divorced working fathers suffer Bad-Daddy Guilt in spades: they are the ultimate "absent" fathers. Not only do they fail to show up for dinner, they fail to show up altogether, at least in the way they used to show up. Now, I am not about to tell any divorced father that he has nothing to feel guilty about toward his children; no one would believe me anyhow. Divorce *is* a dirty deal for the kids, particularly in those early months before new routines are established. Yet we do know that if they try their damnedest to make the best of it, divorced working fathers can still be great, involved fathers and role models to their children. My point here is that one major factor that prevents divorced fathers from being effective fathers is their super dose of guilt. They have a tendency to feel ashamed and apologetic whenever they come in contact with their children. Everything they say and do seems to be prefaced by "I'm sorry I screwed up your life, but . . ." Not good for either parent or child. And definitely no fun. The pitfalls of guilty fathering discussed below apply to all working fathers, but perhaps a bit more so to divorced working dads.

The Guilty-Spoiler Trap

For the third time in a row, you miss Morgan's Little League game after promising him that you'd be there. On the way home from the late-running business meeting that kept you at the office, you stop at a sporting goods store and buy Morgan a brand-new first baseman's mitt. When you get home, you present it to him with your apologies for missing the game. Morgan is sullen as he returns to his room with this token of your guilt.

The above scenario, with variations, undoubtedly accounts for a large part of the current glut of spoiled children. Parental guilt begets spoiling behavior—it always has and it always will. For starters, a father who is forever operating from a position of guilt makes a lousy disciplinarian; he is simply feeling too guilty to say no. Take the above situation: say that later on that evening, Morgan is found watching television when he is supposed to be doing his homework. You know you should say something to him about it, but geez, you've caused the little guy enough grief for one day, right? What you may not realize is that Morgan, even if he is only six years old, knows from experience that when you are feeling guilty he can get away with murder—and that is precisely how spoiling begins. Of course, if you habitually feel guilty, the little guy figures he can get away with murder virtually all of the time.

You know you are in trouble when you notice that you are beginning an inordinate number of communications to your child with, "I'm sorry, but . . ." And inasmuch as everything you do with your child provides her with a model of behavior to emulate, you may soon discover that she is "sorry, but" a great deal of the time herself. She has learned that she can break promises and rules as long as she says "I'm sorry" afterward; she becomes an inveterate excusemaker, just like Dad. Again, the outcome is a spoiled child.

A common variation on the Guilty Spoiler theme is the Big Gesturer, the guilty father who is forever making deals with his children in an attempt to make up for what he cannot or will not do. "I know I didn't read to you at bedtime all week, but next Saturday I'll take you to the circus, front row!" Aside from spoiling the child in the usual way, this bartering approach to time with him—one front-row seat at the circus in exchange for five bedtime stories—has the overall effect of devaluing your day-to-day relationship with your child. Its direct implication is that merely putting him to bed and reading him a story is cheap stuff compared to a trip to the circus. Is it any wonder the child becomes disenchanted when you actually do read to him and put him to bed? Among other things, it means that he has lost a chit in the circus sweepstakes. And so it is spoiled-child time again. (I should note here that the concept of spending Quality Time with your child—which we will discuss in detail in Part II—can all too easily devolve into a bartering situation with the same effects on your child.)

Unhappily, a spoiled child is a menace to herself as well as to those around her. A child without sufficient discipline, without consistent limits, is often an unfocused and unsatisfied child. In addition, she is usually bad company and may find herself without friends who will put up with her spoiled behavior. One all-too-common outcome is that you, her father, may find yourself reflexively avoiding her, because a spoiled child is never a pleasure to be around. Avoiding your own child—now *there's* something to feel really guilty about!

Amazing Child = Fantastic Dad

I have recently noticed the escalation of another unfortunate way that working fathers visit their guilt on their children: by turning them into showpieces. By priming his child with the very best lessons in ballet or gymnastics or the violin or mathematics, and then prodding the child to display his or her talents, this guilty father attempts to prove to himself and others that he is a fantastic parent—witness his amazing child! After all, a kid who is that terrific must be the product of a doting dad, in spite of the fact that Dad doesn't actually spend that much time with his kid.

Of course, the key word here is "product," for clearly this father is treating his child more as a product than as a person with whom he has a relationship. Obviously, both father and child get shortchanged in such an arrangement. I cannot entirely lay this trend of child-as-product at the door of overcompensating, guilty working fathers (and mothers); it is part of a more general trend of expanding personal competition to include one's children. And it is not, of course, an entirely new phenomenon; '50s parents were famous for using their children to be competitive with other parents. ("My Charlie got into Princeton, how about your boy?") Still, I must confess that I find it particularly disappointing that the current crop of parents can be as kid-competitive as their own parents were. So if one step away from this trend is to rid ourselves of Bad-Daddy Guilt, I have another reason to heartily endorse that step.

Circle of Guilt

Let us return, for a moment, to the above scenario wherein you have missed the Little League game but try to make up for it by buying your son an expensive gift, a new baseball mitt. Recall that the boy's response was less than enthusiastic—a bit sullen, in fact. What is going on here?

The boy is feeling guilty, that's what. Yes, he likes the mitt you got him just fine, but his overriding feeling is disappointment because you did not come to the game as you promised you would. The emotional result is that he does not feel particularly appreciative of your gift or your reason for presenting it to him, yet in the next moment he feels bad about feeling and acting so underwhelmed by your generosity. He *feels* like he is a spoiled, unappreciative brat, and that makes him feel guilty.

What Guilty Dad has done here is to pass along his own guilt. He may even unconsciously advance the process by pushing a guilt button or two in his child. *"Hey, give me a break, will you, Morgan? It's not like I was out having fun when I missed your game. I was working my ass off so I can buy things like this mitt for you—so how about lightening up, huh?"* That will definitely give his boy's incipient guilt a good push.

The psychological mechanism operating here is the mistaken (and unconscious) assumption that if you manage to get your son feeling guilty, it will somehow lighten your own load of guilt. Not so. In fact, the more likely outcome is that you will feel guilty for making him feel guilty—thereby completing the circle of guilt.

The "Little Man" Syndrome

While we are on the subject of burdening our children with guilt, I would like to make at least a passing reference to a current phenomenon in child rearing that I find particularly disturbing: communicating to our little children *all* of our feelings, including our disappointments and frustrations. ("Boy, did I have rotten day, Morgan. It looks like I'm not going to get that assignment I wanted and that makes me feel like a failure.") This is done in the spirit of openness and is, I suspect, a reaction to the relative emotional secretiveness of our own parents. (It is also frequently done by single parents who simply need someone to talk to at the end of the day.) I have had parents tell me that they believe their "little man" is learning how to be a good listener and how to understand grown-ups' problems. ("It's important for them to find out that we aren't perfect, that we have troubles too.") But in my experience, laying all this emotional baggage on our kids is not good for them at all; it simply makes them feel less secure about their parents than they should be feeling. And furthermore, it can load them with plenty of guilt, because they sense that their parents are asking them to make *them* feel better, and these little guys cannot possibly know how to do that. If you feel the need to unburden yourself, that is what good friends—and psychotherapists—are there for.

Guilt and Avoidance

I mentioned earlier how a father can find himself avoiding his very own spoiled child because this whiny, demanding kid is not very good company—especially at the end of a taxing day at the office. But that is not the only way that guilt induces us to avoid our children. At base, we are rather simple beings who reflexively avoid pain and discomfort whenever and however it presents itself. Thus, if we have gotten ourselves into a state of mind where we habitually feel guilty for being a Bad Daddy, we will instinctively avoid anything that reminds us of that guilt—*like the very children whom we feel guilty about not spending enough time with!* If this sounds crazy, you are right—but that does not mean it does not happen frequently, creating a cycle of avoidance and guilt for avoidance that spirals ever downward.

What's a Dad to Do?

The answer to this question is the same basic resolution that runs throughout this book: be conscious and be clear to everyone around you. If you know your own priorities and trust your judgment to pick them out as alternatives present themselves, you will not feel constantly torn between them, *nor will you feel guilty for choosing one or the other at any particular time.*

If Morgan's Little League games usually conflict with your

work demands, pick out only those games that are especially important to attend (say, the finals) and make special arrangements at work ahead of time so that you can definitely be there. In other words, *don't feel guilty for doing the best you can.*

Above all, *don't make promises to your kids that there is any likelihood you will not be able to keep.* If you know you have a meeting that starts at 4 P.M. and you know these meetings sometimes run overtime, don't even suggest to Morgan that you might make it to the game. If it turns out that you can be there, terrific! It will be a great surprise for him. But if you say you are coming and do not, you just disappoint him and prime the guilt machine.

As for that clingy Bad-Daddy Guilt, be as aware of it (in all its clever disguises) as you can. And resist its powerful push in the direction of kid-spoiling behavior.

Bad-Hubby Guilt

Bad-Hubby Guilt is a growth industry. On the one hand, we feel guilty toward our wives for not pulling our fair share of the workload at home; and on the other, we feel guilty for not paying enough attention—sexual and otherwise—to our wives because we are so overwhelmed by our workload both at home and at work.

Although traditionally men have been all too willing to let women do the lion's share of housework and child-care duties, men also have a tradition of not wanting to let teammates down, of feeling bad when we let co-workers pick up the slack for us. And now that men are acknowledging that we and our working wives are co-workers on the home front, we really do feel guilty when we let them down.

The solution, of course, is to not let them down, to work things out equitably so you have nothing to feel guilty about. Easier said than done, of course, but again, this is addressed in detail in Part II. In the meantime, there's still that Bad-Hubby Guilt to contend with, along with all of its fallout.

"I'm Sorry, So Sorry . . ."

Until you've worked out an equitable way of sharing home tasks with your wife (and often, even afterward), Bad-Hubby Guilt can promote a truly sorry relationship. "I'm sorry I didn't pick up the cleaning, but by the time I got there they were closed." "I'm sorry I screwed up dressing Milly for school, but I couldn't find her blue sneakers." "I'm sorry, but can you trade taking Milly to the dentist tomorrow for taking her next week?"

Your working wife is often full of apologies too, so the two of you are constantly sorry, forever asking each other for forgiveness and indulgence and another chance. This may all be very empathetic and compassionate, but I can assure you that it does not make for a very dynamic or joyful relationship. Two people in perpetual apologetic mode are two people who never completely connect with each other. Among other things, it is not very sexy.

And Speaking of Not Very Sexy . . .

A rather common problem in families of two working parents is that sex gets crowded out of your life along with golf and the poker night. The solution to this may not strike you as particularly romantic, but it sure beats the hell out of abstinence: *schedule it!* (More about this in Part II.)

But in the meantime, be forewarned that the guilt and frustration you feel for not making love to your wife as often as either of you would like can seriously poison your relationship. You may find yourself going to the other extreme, from sorriness to blame. You become convinced that she never makes enough time for sex with you and you tell her so accusingly. You find yourself thinking that she doesn't turn you on anymore, but the fact is that when you are finally alone with her at night, you're too tired to feel turned on by Isabella Rossellini. On top of the guilt you feel toward your wife, not having sex with her tends to make you feel generally less sexually confident—which, in turn, can make you feel guilty toward yourself. ("I'm not the man I used to be. What am I doing to myself?") And, of course, one possible outcome of low sexual confidence is a good dose of performance anxiety on those rare occasions when you and your wife do get around to being in bed and awake at the same time.

"Oh, Yeah, and How Are You?"

As our schedules get increasingly crowded, another (and subtler) form of guilt we feel toward our wives is that of simply not being there emotionally for her. ("Remember when we used to talk at the end of the day?" "I can't remember the last time we just held hands on the sofa.") This, of course, cuts both ways: our working wives are not the companions and confidantes and comforting huggers they were before the children came along and/or before they started working full-time too.

There is one main thing I want to say about this guilt: *pay it heed, brother!* If your wife (and perhaps you too) is not getting sufficient emotional fulfillment from your marriage because intimacy has become a casualty of your working-father time-binds and exhaustion, your marriage could be heading for serious trouble. And just feeling guilty about that won't help at all. You need to do what you need to do to nip that guilt—and its cause—in the bud.

A couple, Will and Jenny, came to see me after each had been ignoring his/her Bad-Partner Guilt for far too long. One reason they had been able to disregard their guilt over not being there for each other is that they had started to believe their own publicity as the "perfect couple." Indeed, on paper their lives were impressive: she is a pediatrician with a flourishing practice; he is a hospital administrator responsible for five hundred employees. In addition to their professional lives, each is heavily involved in community affairs—he coaches bas-

ketball and is on the board of the local Red Cross and the
YMCA; she is on a school committee and leads a women's
discussion group. On top of all of this, with the help of nannies
and baby-sitters, they are raising two wonderful children.
When Will and Jenny appear at a public function—which they
often do—people gaze at them in wonder. Yes, indeed, the
perfect couple. Except that when they came into my office,
they had not made love in three months.

"We just never seem to be crawling into bed at the same
time," Jenny said.

"Or when we do, we're both too tired to do more than give
each other a peck and crash." Will sighed. "I feel kind of
guilty about it, but there it is."

"Thank God you do feel guilty about it," I said. "You
should. And I bet you feel more than just guilty—you both
probably feel a little lonely too. I mean, I know you are involved all day with your patients and employees and your
children, but if you are not getting any real one-on-one intimacy with your mate—and I don't just mean sexual intimacy—
you can start to feel terribly lonely. And that's when things
begin to fall apart."

I think it was at about this point in my little speech that
Jenny started to weep. I stopped talking. Will got out of his
chair and threw his arms around his wife; they held each other
very tightly for a few minutes and then Will said, "I think it's
time to reorganize our lives."

"Yes, it is," Jenny agreed.

"End of therapy session," I said after a moment, rising. "I
think you both know what to do now."

Bad-Worker Guilt

Here, feel free to substitute the word "panic" for "guilt"
whenever the spirit moves you. Because the *guilt* you feel for
not producing the same *quality* of work that you did before
you started doing your fair share at home . . . and the *guilt*

you feel for not producing the same *quantity* of work . . . and the *guilt* you feel every time you have to say No to the boss . . . and the *guilt* you feel every time your co-workers have to pick up your slack . . . and the *guilt* you feel every time you screw up an assignment because you are feeling so overwhelmed you can't think straight . . . all of that *guilt* sure as hell feels like *panic* most of the time.

Guilt and panic have something else in common in this context: they both can make you into one very unattractive worker. Whether you deal with your guilt by being eternally apologetic ("God, I'm sorry this report is so ragged, but . . .") or by being hyperdefensive ("Get off my back, will ya? I'm doing the best that I can"), the impression you will make at work is of a man who is not in control of his life. Whatever other failings you may have, this is the one that can do your reputation at the office the worst damage: the best jobs do not go to a man who appears to be out of control.

Here is where the circle of guilt again expands. If you are fairing poorly at work as a result of your guilty behavior, you may automatically blame your family for these failures. ("I didn't get the Andersen assignment because I had to miss too many meetings last week in order to take Milly to her ballet lessons.") And the result can be that both your hardworking wife and Milly start feeling guilty for bolixing up your professional life, even though it is really the manner in which *you* handled the situation that accounts for your low standing at the office.

Bad-Friend Guilt

Let's face it, in the grand calculus of the working dad's time, friends and charities get dropped first. Out with volunteering for the Red Cross, goodbye Thursday night poker games and Saturday morning golf games, and so long to unwinding over beers with a couple of buddies in a bar—you've got places to go and things to do . . . and so do little Milly and Johnny.

This feels bad enough in itself—after all, you are depriving yourself of one of your treasured pleasures in life, male companionship. But then your single and childless friends start making comments like, "I remember when you were still fun," and your married-with-children friends who *haven't* sacrificed friend-time to work-and-family time start making comments like, "Wimp!" That is when Bad-Friend Guilt—and Bad-Friend Anger—rear their ugly heads.

Interestingly, Bad-Friend Guilt, minor as it may appear in comparison with Bad-Daddy, Bad-Husband, or Bad-Worker Guilt, can be the guilt that breaks the camel's back. A man says no to his friends one time too many and he feels his life suddenly caving in on him. ("God, is life all travail and zero fun?") What is more, the avoiding-the-source-of-guilt phenomenon can kick in here too: you find yourself avoiding your friends because you know you'll just have to decline their invitations and that will make you feel guilty—so you avoid them and *that* makes you feel guilty. It's a downward spiral.

Here, again, the answer lies in time management, a subject we will work hard on in Part II. But let me just say here that I believe it is a bad idea to opt out of your male friendships— bad for you, bad for your family, and bad for your co-workers. Because a man without friends and without recreation is a joyless father, husband, and teammate. The solution is in a balanced life; believe me, there is time enough in every Marathon Dad's schedule for an occasional round of beers with a few friends. It will not only balance your life but keep some of that guilt away.

Unfulfillment Guilt

A man who frantically tries to fulfill the overwhelming demands of work and family may look at himself and say, "What happened to all my dreams? To everything I was going to accomplish? Am I earning what I should be at my age? Do I have all the material things I wanted? Am I taking the professional risks I promised myself I would? Or have I sacrificed it all to be someone else's idea of a fulfilled husband and father?"

Or he may look at himself and say, "God, has my world shrunk! I have no spiritual life left. No intellectual life. Not even any physical life. It's all work and duties, but what's happened to *me*?"

Or he may look at himself and say, "Look at me! I'm not a man anymore—I'm some kind of feminized homebody!"

Or, like his counterpart, the working mother, he may look at himself and say, "Other people seem to do it all, so why can't I?"

Whatever the variations of disappointment and self-incrimination, the end result is the same: guilt directed at one-self. It is the guilt of failure, of unfulfilled promise, of disloy-alty to one's earlier and "better" self. This guilt can do serious damage to our sense of self and self-esteem. In the process, it can rob us of our humor, plunge us into depression, and bleed us of energy. Bad stuff, all of it, and not to be trifled with.

The answer here is not simply better time management, although that is part of the solution. In order not to feel guilty toward ourselves, we have to be fully conscious of the priorit-ies we set and the choices we make, *and then we have to own our choices.* A man who knows exactly why he has made the trade-offs in his life that he has is a man who does not feel guilty about them. Again, simpler said than done. But we will address in detail the best ways to consciously set our priorities and make peace with them in Part II.

7

Hidden Hurdles at Home

▼ ▼ ▼ ▼

Ambivalent Wives and the
"Can't-Win-for-Losing" Problem

*Y*ou're upstairs bathing little Stevie, the two of you laughing
like idiots as you nose-dive Rubber Ducky into the tub, splash-
ing water in each other's faces, on your shirt, and onto the
floor. Suddenly behind you, the bathroom door opens: it is
your wife. You find yourself smiling to yourself because you
know how pleased she will be; here you are, not only spending
time with your child but doing one of those drudge tasks that
she used to accuse you of shirking. You turn to your wife
expectantly.

"It doesn't look like he's getting very clean," she intones
soberly, as she steps closer to inspect behind Stevie's ears.

What, you may ask, is going on here?

In a word, *sabotage!* Although she has probably done it
unconsciously, your wife has effectively undermined your role
as father. She has called into question both your skills and
your intent as a bather of children—and right in front of your
son, who believes it must be true. Why would she do such a
thing, even unconsciously? After all, this is the very same
woman who has been encouraging you for years to pull your
fair share of the load at home. Well, one reason is because
you and Stevie were having far too much fun up there, a dead

giveaway that you are treating your task frivolously. But there are deeper reasons lurking beneath the surface here, and these reasons deserve our close attention because they are clues to a number of hurdles to successful fatherhood that our wives may be unwittingly setting in our way.

What follows is not a litany of blame, but a call for understanding. Above all, Marathon Dad needs to do his part to unhinge the Battle of the Sexes, to reveal lingering stereotypes and fears in their historical contexts so that we can move on to a new era of Complementarity of the Sexes.

Super Mom's Four Greatest Fears

Certainly our wives really do want us to contribute more at home now that they are working too. And they think it would be good for the children if we had closer and steadier relationships with them. But just like us, our wives are burdened with myths and stereotypes, fears and guilts, that can cause them to send us mixed messages, messages that say, in effect, *"Do your fair share, honey, but remember, home is my turf!"*

These messages spring from a variety of mom motives and are expressed in a variety of subtle and not-so-subtle ways. But from wherever they spring and however they are expressed, they are supremely counterproductive for *both* Dad and Mom, steering us away from the cooperation and interdependence that would make life easier and more fulfilling for us and our children.

Fear #1: We'll Screw Up

One place these messages come from is our wives' genuine fear that we will foul up every family task we take on because of our inexperience and inherent oafishness. These women have bought into the twin ideas that men mysteriously turn into idiots around the house and that, anyway, keeping house and raising children are on a par with neurosurgery when it comes to the necessary knowledge and skills. As a result, they are convinced that not only will we not bathe little Stevie, satisfactorily, but we are likely to incur a life-threatening accident in the process. Both of these fears can prey so heavily on these moms that they end up insisting on giving Stevie his baths themselves—and thereby teaching him the mythology of the Incompetent Dad so that he can go on to become one himself.

Of course, this is not fair to anyone involved, including little Stevie who rather likes being bathed by his father—for one reason, because it *is* more fun. It is not fair to Dad, who probably is getting to like bath time himself, but who does not like being treated as if he is a nincompoop, especially in front of his young son. And finally, it is not fair to Mom herself, because it binds her to yet one more home task that she could shed, giving her more time for her job, other home duties, or just for herself.

Are these moms' fears realistic? Not really. First, most of us are willing to admit that Stevie probably will come out of the tub less squeaky-clean than if Mom had done the honors; but it is not as if he will come out of the tub with a case of impetigo. This is a prime example of Mom setting mom standards for our tasks; if we don't live up to them, she jumps to the conclusion that we must be doing the job seriously wrong. *Wrong.* We are simply doing it our way, which may not be up to her exacting standards, but it ain't so bad either. Getting this fully understood around the house is one of the prerequisites for establishing that home revolution in attitudes that we know as "A Dad Is Not a Mom."

Mom's fear of life-threatening accidents is a more delicate problem. Every time she hears little Steve squealing in the upstairs bathroom, she is convinced he is going under for the last time. In fact, it is true that fathers tend to be more casual caregivers than moms; and it is even true that kids are more likely to suffer *minor* accidents when in their fathers' care than in their mothers' (chiefly because they are more likely to engage in rough-and-tumble games). But I have never seen any data that suggests that kids are more likely to be seriously or fatally injured in their father's care than in their mother's. And for her to believe otherwise is to be irrational.

So how should we respond when Mom walks into the bathroom and moans that Stevie doesn't look particularly clean, or when Mom flies into the bathroom in a panic because she thinks that Stevie is drowning?

We should quietly but *firmly* assure her that everything is just fine, thank you. If we do that enough times, and if Stevie miraculously survives all these baths moderately clean and in good health, the home revolution will have been advanced one more step. Note that it is important that we be on guard against our *own* temptation to use Mom's fear as an excuse for getting out of child care. (*"Hey, I'd really like to give Stevie his baths, but Louise gets so upset because I don't get him clean that I stay downstairs and read the newspaper and let her do it."*)

Fear #2: She'll Lose Her Crown as the Queen of Home Life

Just as we have a long legacy of fatherhood handed down to us, our wives have a long legacy of motherhood that includes their traditional role as Queen of House, the accepted expert who ultimately makes all the basic decisions on how things should be done at home. In the recent past, this was the source of Mom's basic identity and her fundamental power. She determined everything from what the kids wore to what everyone ate, from what kind of washing machine was purchased to how the home was decorated.

Let's face it, no matter how ambitious and successful today's mom has become in her professional life, and no matter how overworked and fatigued she may feel at the end of the day, this is not the kind of status or power that *anyone* relinquishes gladly. But once our wives start sharing the home workload with us, they inevitably have to give up some of that status and power. A Marathon Dad who, say, now makes the dinners or who does the laundry on alternate weekends is very likely to establish a new family menu or to decide that a different kind of washer would be more efficient. Next thing you know, he's suggesting changes in the living room decor—say more corduroy and less chintz—and the former Queen of All Things Domestic is starting to feel a large part of her identity beginning to unravel.

Mom's fear here has a competitive edge: if Mom and Dad are suddenly equals at home while Dad still enjoys a number of historically male advantages in the workplace, Mom has lost the one place where she held undisputed superior status. That cannot feel good. Thus it provides one hell of a motive for holding on to the notion of Dad-the-Incompetent, the guy who needs the resident expert, Mom, to supervise everything he does around the house or, when you get right down to it, to do it herself.

From this motive springs the kind of wifely ambivalence that is guaranteed to make the whole family unhappy. She may express this ambivalence by performing a household task that we dads have already committed to doing ourselves—and then claiming that she was tired of waiting for us to do it. Or, she usurps one of our household jobs because, she says, judging by the way we did it the last time, she'd have to do it again anyhow. Another way she may express this ambivalence is by switching priorities on us, as in the following scenario that I experienced: I am in the middle of the kitchen, preparing a lasagna, when my wife comes in and says petulantly, "I thought you said you were going to do the laundry today."

This kind of communication is not conducive to a cooperative atmosphere, to say the least. Again, we Marathon Dads have to take a firm but reasonable stand against such messages. It is one of those issues that we need to talk about with our wives on a regular basis. Don't quote me on this, but it's for their own good as much as for ours.

I had one patient, a thirty-seven-year-old man named Stephen, who had gotten into the habit of letting his wife, Allie, make virtually all the decisions about how to raise their two-year-old, Brian. To begin with, Stephen was predisposed to distrusting fathers in general because his own father had been so abusive (this was the main reason Stephen had entered therapy in the first place), so he looked to women for the right way to be a parent; but in addition to that, Allie was a psychotherapist, so he considered her an "expert" on child rearing.

When Allie departed for a five-day conference on the other side of the country, she left a list on the refrigerator door that detailed exactly how to take care of Brian—everything from how deep and hot his bathwater should be to the precise hour and regime of his bedtime. As it turned out, Stephen had a pressing deadline in his work (he is a freelance sound editor whose studio is attached to their house). So when Brian refused to stay in bed, even though his dad had followed the precise bedtime routine written down on The List, Stephen started to lose it. He called me at home in a panic. "I don't know what I did wrong," he told me. "I did everything on The List."

"Maybe that's the problem," I responded.

"What do you mean?"

"It's Allie's list, not yours. Little kids have a terrific capacity for knowing when a parent is doing something because it feels right to him and when he's doing something because he's following somebody else's directions. Tell you what. Go to the refrigerator, take down the list, and tear it into little pieces. You've got four days to go before your wife comes back, so start now taking care of Brian in your *own* way."

Stephen was hesitant. "Well, what if I brought a futon into the studio and let him play while I got some work done?"

"Sounds like a plan."

"But I don't think Allie would approve."

"Allie's in California," I said.

Stephen's plan worked out wonderfully: he got his work done, his little son had the treat of dozing off in his dad's studio, and no harm was done. Yet when Allie came home and found out about this deviation from The List, she was very unhappy. "We're giving Brian double messages," she told her husband.

"He seems to be coping okay," Stephen replied.

"Well, I wish you had consulted me before you started changing things," Allie persisted.

It was at this point that Stephen had an epiphany of sorts: he realized it wasn't just his own insecurities that had made his wife into the "expert" parent; she had a lot invested in that role herself. Except that now, after four successful days of fathering on his own, Stephen didn't feel the same need for Allie to be the expert. He had come smack up against Fear #2.

There is another competitive element that often comes into play here: our wives' fear that we will turn out to be as good at being a parent as they are. Mom is used to being the most dependable, devoted, and caring parent in the children's eyes, but now that we dads are picking up Samantha at school and giving Stevie his bath, Mom has to share the children's allegiance and affection more equitably than ever before. Again, this goes against the grain of tradition and can result—albeit unwittingly—in a running competition with Dad to be the Favorite Parent. I am not surprised when I see this dynamic at play between divorced parents, but it is alarming how often I see married couples vying with one another for "points" with the kids. Like any competition between parents, it does not lead the way to cooperation. And, perhaps worse, it keeps us from recognizing that our roles are complementary, that it takes a dad *and* a mom to do the best job of all.

Fear #3: We Are Always up to Something Sneaky

Unfortunately, one male stereotype that clings to us even as we try to become more fair-minded marriage partners is the notion that we men are basically untrustworthy, that no matter what we appear to be doing, we are really operating on some nefarious agenda. Every ugly statistic on deadbeat dads or news story about a father abandoning his family serves to heighten this fear in some women. And it immediately gets translated into suspicion: *"He says he'll take care of the kids while I go out with my friends—but what's he really after now?"*

A related motivating force here may be some women's investment in their anger as an integral part of their identity. Remember, it was genuine, well-justified anger that aided many women in their fight to make society and the workplace fairer places for women. That anger and its accompanying suspicion have kept them alert to injustices and, yes, to the sneaky ways many men and male institutions have tried to hold on to their power. Letting go of this anger and suspicion can feel to them like letting down their guard, a step backward to subjugation.

But again, to reach the point of true equality and efficient interdependence at home, that anger and suspicion need to be given a rest. And there is only one way we can help our wives reach that point: *by being consistently trustworthy. And by keeping our cool in the process.*

As we men approach the problem of combining our professional lives with our family lives, we have one major advantage that the women pioneers in this realm did not have: we are not, in general, burdened with as much anger as these women historically brought with them. Although we may feel loads of resentment about the way some of the rules of family life are changing in mid-game, we are not seething over a history of injustice. We can use this relative cool to lead the entire family to a more balanced, less ideological, and more practical approach to the problems of combining work and family.

Fear #4: The More Domesticated We Become, the Less Sexy We'll Be

A woman I know who is an ardent feminist and a consummate professional made the following confession to me:

"My husband and I had been working hard at making things fairer around the house and, like most men, [he] was a little slow to grasp just how much work there was for us to share. Well, one evening I came home from the office to find him washing the dishes in an apron. This is a scene I'd been dreaming about for years—and so what is my first reaction? I find myself thinking—Yuck, am I going to bed tonight with a guy who wears an apron?"

Of course, this woman was much more conscious and honest than most people, but she did shed light on an area of the female unconscious that can work against job-sharing at home. The sad truth is that, just as the office is becoming a sexier place since more women arrive there, home seems to be becoming a less sexy place. In large part, this is because we now have two working people trying to schedule relaxed time together; but the other part is that our libidos are having a problem catching up with the new image of a Real Man and a Real Woman. And so, like my friend, many women find it hard to reconcile the idea of a guy in an apron with the masculine lover of their dreams. (Similarly, it is difficult for many men to reconcile the idea of a gal carrying a hard hat or a bulging attaché case with the feminine lover of their dreams.)

The result, again, can be some kind of unconscious sabotage. Not really knowing that it is her husband's apparent feminization that is making her feel so uncomfortable, the wife who comes home to find him in an apron may find herself anxiously criticizing the way he scours the saucepan. Talk about not winning for losing—what's a well-meaning guy to do?

Well, for starters, we all—men and women—need to accept the fact that when it comes to the unconscious and to sexual attractiveness, reason and ideology are powerless. As I mentioned, the woman who made the above confession to me was a feminist, but she was wise enough to understand that some part of her libido was beyond the reaches of political correctness. So my basic solution is quite simple: *give her libido (and your self-image) a break—don't wear an apron when you do the dishes—at least not a frilly one!* I am being serious. Because what we have here is one more reason for doing household and caregiving tasks in a distinctly male way, one more reason for completely embracing the idea that Daddy is not Mommy.

Hidden Hurdles in Society

▼ ▼ ▼ ▼

Macho Media–Legacies and Alibis

The media, that great shaper of stereotypes and popular assumptions, influence not only how we perceive the role of fathers today but how we view the legacy of fatherhood that has been handed down to us. By absorbing these assumptions along with everyone else who watches TV and reads magazines and popular books, we are once again prone to unconsciously narrowing our options of how to be a successful Marathon Dad.

Consider the way we think about our *own* fathers, the '50s dads. On the one hand, we remember these fathers through the rosy-farcical filter of sit-com reruns of *Father Knows Best, Leave It to Beaver,* and *The Wonder Years,* which made them out to be well-meaning oafs who were too preoccupied and inherently inept to do anything useful around the house. On the other hand, we recall these '50s dads through today's pop-psychology revisionist filter of books and magazine articles which make them out to be driven, emotionally retarded, macho types whose sole contributions to our upbringing were to foot the grocery bills and to lower our self-esteem. What are we supposed to do with either of these images when we attempt to acknowledge our place in the Historical Legacy of Fatherhood?

The poet Robert Bly has urged us to make peace with our own fathers, to recognize what they gave to us that we want to pass on to our own children—a goal I heartily endorse. But to get to a place where we can do so honestly and comfortably, we need to disabuse ourselves of some of these stock appraisals of '50s dads. Was Dad really as incompetent and oafish as Robert Young (*Father Knows Best*) would have us believe? Or was he simply never given the opportunity to try his hand at a whole spectrum of roles and tasks around the house because these roles and tasks were "off-limits?" Was he really as cold and strict as many contemporary psychotherapists would have us believe? Or was he stymied from demonstrating deep-felt emotions by the protocols and expectations of the day?

It turns out that most of us have been handed a revisionist view of our fathers that does not give them their due, mostly because it does not see them in their historic context. This revisionist view maintains that '50s Dad distanced himself from the family *on purpose* because he was afraid of family feelings (or feelings of any kind, for that matter), because he was monomaniacal about professional accomplishment and so was barely conscious of his family's very existence, and because in his macho heart he did not believe that home was a man's place even if it was his castle.

Really? For starters, what this view leaves out is the fundamental fact that during this period Dad worked and Mom did not, which meant, among other things, that Dad was solely responsible for keeping the family financially afloat. In fact, surveys show that most '50s fathers took this responsibility very seriously, that it weighed heavily upon them, and that this sense of responsibility accounted for their absence from the family (both physically and emotionally) more than either their ego-driven ambition or their so-called natural aversion to family feelings. The same surveys show that a majority of these fathers actually *craved more family contact* but were unable to indulge this craving for fear of shirking their primary responsibility to the family. What we find, then, is a generation of men who saw their fatherhood roles first and foremost as *Providers* and *Protectors*—valued roles that too often become obscured by our reflexive critique of them as *Withholders of Love* and *Strict Disciplinarians*. Further, it is not as if these dads totally eschewed the fatherhood roles of *Nurturer* and *Teacher*—these roles were simply given second billing in their minds, largely because they had less time for them, not less desire.

We should also remember that '50s Dad had little support in expanding his role to include emotional intimacy with his children. In fact, one person who often worked hard at excluding him from this role was none other than his spouse, '50s Mom. Without a career, '50s Mom's entire identity was wrapped up in her home and children, in being the Queen of Nurture; therefore, she guarded her turf jealously and often (no doubt unconsciously) pushed '50s Dad into roles that would guarantee him limited intimacy with the children. I am thinking, for example, of that famous '50s phenomenon of Mom chillingly saying to a naughty child, "Wait until your father comes home!"—a sure way to keep the kids intimidated by Dad and hence emotionally removed from him.

Living with the Sins of Our Fathers

A number of unfortunate outcomes can occur when we uncritically accept a revisionist view of '50s Dad. Consider, for example, the myth that he was *willfully* cold and removed from his children. This myth goes a long way to bolster the currently popular idea that we men have a major inborn problem getting in touch with and showing our feelings. The daughters of '50s fathers have been heavily promoting this idea ever since I can remember. Now, one piece that has followed from this idea is the '90s notion that we men *need to get in touch with our feminine side*. The assumption here, of course, is that feelings are by their very nature feminine (how's that for sexism?), so if we are going to have any genuine, deep feelings, we have to make like women—to become emotional cross-dressers. The next step is all too predictable: if we are going to be feeling, nurturing fathers, we need to make like mothers. As we saw in the section called "A Dad Is Not A Mom," this kind of thinking can create a serious hurdle to becoming a successful Marathon Dad.

Another way that these '50s myths of Macho Dad come around and hit us in the face in the '90s is the equation of *all* masculine behavior with insensitive family behavior. Somehow, merely playing a round of golf or watching a football game with a beer in hand is deemed destructive to the family simply because it is a "guy" thing. This can happen even if we have put in a fair share of time and emotion being full-partner dads. It's the alleged sins of the fathers doing us in again, and we may find ourselves "atoning" for those sins by giving up that round of golf or that afternoon in front of the TV set—and then, of course, resenting the entire family for it.

One couple I was seeing, Greg and Julie, had to sort themselves out of this particular confusion. When they first came to see me, Greg was doing much less than his equal share of child and home care, even though his wife's job was every bit as demanding as his. In our sessions he kept saying he wanted to change, but he had a load of bad habits to overcome. Well, in a matter of a half year, Greg was able to throw out virtually all of those bad habits and become a fully involved and fair-minded working parent and partner. I saw the change and so did Julie. Yet she still felt that Greg was holding out on her.

"He's still doing his macho thing," she complained. "You know, still going out after work for a drink with his cronies and acting like a frat-house jerk."

"Does that prevent him from doing the tasks you both decided he would do?"

"No, but that's not the point," Julie insisted. "It just seems to me that when you get married and have a job and kids, it's time to give up that juvenile stuff."

"You mean, it doesn't conform to your *image* of a married man with a job and kids."

"Exactly," Julie agreed. "It's just so—you know—retro."

"No," I countered. "A married man who doesn't pull his fair share of the load at home is retro. But a married man who still enjoys the company of other men in a saloon is simply a man who knows what he likes."

Julie was not happy with my analysis; she accused me of siding with her husband on a "guy" issue. But at the next session, she confessed that after thinking about it, she realized she had been "mixing up form with content" on the "saloon thing."

Unfortunately, we men have been known to use '50s mythology to sabotage our own goals of being successful Marathon Dads. Too often I have seen dads portraying themselves as sitcom like, charming, incompetent oafs who defer to their wives as domestic experts—and as a result, get out of such onerous tasks as changing diapers or wiping the high chair clean. It is a comfortable role, always good for a few laughs when we botch up some simple domestic task to keep our oafish reputation alive. Obviously, this does not charm a working mother as much as it may have Mrs. Cleaver; in point of fact, it is just an alibi for shirking our fair share of the workload. One variation on this particular delusion that I have seen quite a bit of lately is the father who says, "Usually I would change Gabriel's diaper, but he's a little feverish today and needs his mother." If one looks closely, we see that *every* day has extenuating circumstances for this kind of father; he is just a recycled version of the sitcom incompetent oaf—Dagwood with '90s double-talk.

Perhaps the most common way we use '50s Dad stereotypes to keep ourselves from becoming competent and fulfilled Marathon Dads is by comparing ourselves to these mythic fathers and finding ourselves simply wonderful by comparison. "Hey, I'm so much more helpful, loving, and involved with the kids than my father was, I'm a real gift." The implication, of course, is that everybody should be satisfied with how much this father contributes on the home front; even if it is not precisely an equal share, it is still a hell of a lot more than the norm used to be. (Of course, this attitude conveniently dismisses the fact that this was the norm at a time when Mom did not work outside the home.) This is no more than a gentrified variation on the old redneck, "Hey, I'm not cheating on my wife, don't drink, gamble, or beat the bejesus out of her—she's got one hell of a deal here!"

'50s Dad, Warts and All

I do not want to push too far in the other direction and create a new myth of '50s Dad as some poor, misunderstood, emotional guy who never got a chance to be the father he really wanted to be. Even if that is a more accurate picture of his emotional makeup than we have been handed by the revisionists, this dad's effect on us, his sons, was still probably to make us feel excluded, unloved, and inferior. Nonetheless, what is important for us now that we are fathers ourselves is to see our own fathers in full dimension so that we can decide what parts of his legacy we want to keep and what parts we want to jettison or change. In other words, I am definitely not saying that we should consciously model ourselves on our own '50s fathers (we've already done that unconsciously), just that we should look at them very clearly, without any prejudice that has seeped into our brains via stereotypes, and draw from them what feels right for our revised model of fatherhood.

For example, most of us still want to hold on to our legacy roles as *Providers* and *Protectors*. With our wives working and providing a substantial part of the family income, these may be roles that we now share with our spouses; but that does not mean that we have to stop identifying with these traditional roles, that we have to throw them out with some outdated '50s model of fatherhood. On the other hand, today we are unwilling to frustrate our yearning for emotional intimacy with our children, unwilling to give second billing to our roles as *Nurturers* and *Teachers*. Perhaps emotional intimacy with our kids is a luxury that was denied our '50s fathers, but we will not deny it to ourselves.

One final thought here. Looking over studies of the differences between '50s fathers and today's fathers, I noticed that '50s fathers saw themselves as spending one to two hours a day with their children, while today's fathers saw themselves spending double that number of hours. (Both figures are undoubtedly exaggerations of the facts.) But what struck me as more significant than the relative number of hours spent with children was the relative *predictability* of those hours. Fifties fathers' time with the kids was much more consistent: he came home from work at the same time every day; his weekend and vacation schedules were also uniform and dependable. By contrast, time with today's dads (and moms too) is less dependable and this can have unfortunate consequences for the children, as we will explore in detail when we discuss scheduling Marathon Dad's time. The reason I mention this fact here is that it is an example of one concrete way we may want to emulate our own fathers' way of fathering.

New Stereotypes for Old

Stereotypes of '90s Super Dads are currently coming at us fast and furious, causing just as much confusion as the old stereotypes do. Consider the following scenario of a popular TV commercial:

We see the young father slipping gracefully into a seat in the school auditorium, boyishly handsome in his business suit with his tie askew. He is late—the performance of kids dressed up as dancing vegetables is already in progress. His eager eyes survey the stage and then he turns to his lovely wife and asks in a whisper, "Which one is she?" His wife smiles. "The asparagus," she replies.

The father portrayed here is busy as hell, but because he

runs like crazy and because he wouldn't miss his kid's performance for the world, he makes it in the nick of time. We are supposed to like this guy, admire his energy and his devotion. He is the adman's model for the fin de siècle father who can do it all.

But just one moment here: *this guy didn't even know his kid was the asparagus, for God's sake!* Where was he when his daughter came home excitedly to announce that she landed the plum asparagus part in the school pageant? If this was the first he knew about it, I sure find it hard to summon up any admiration for his energy and devotion. It reminds me of my reaction to the Woody Allen child-custody trial. I was really trying to hang in there with Woody despite some of his seriously bad behavior and despite the fact that my wife was ready to give him the death penalty. I figured that in spite of everything, Woody had tried his level best to be a good, concerned father to his children; at least that is the way he came off in his testimony. And then one day the defense attorney casually asked Woody the name of his kid's second-grade teacher and Woody didn't have a clue. *What?* He doesn't know his kid's teacher's name and he's claiming to be a concerned, hands-on dad? At that moment I was ready to throw Woody to the dogs, along with the Doesn't-Know-from-Asparagus guy.

It is interesting to speculate on what the adman thought he was conveying when he stuck on the, "Which one is she?" tag line. My guess is he was trying to soothe the guilt of all the fathers out there who don't have a clue about a lot of things in their children's lives, yet who still want to think of themselves as concerned dads. Here, then, is the prevailing media stereotype of the '90s Terrific Dad: breathlessly heroic as he tries to do everything, but gosh, give the guy a break, he cannot do all that and still know what his child's day-to-day life is like. I don't think I need to make a detailed analysis of just how counterproductive that stereotype is for anyone who seriously wants to be a successful Marathon Dad.

A popular variation on this media stereotype is "Techno

Dad," the '90s father who has found a truly modern way to be in two places at the same time: electronically. Most often, he is portrayed on TV showing his concern by calling home on a cell phone from an intense business meeting or, my favorite, faxing his wife a mash note from his seat on an airplane as we see gauzy images of his wife and young daughter awakening at home without him. The clear implication of the latter ad is that this concerned husband/father is even more darling electronically than he would be in the flesh.

I am not a Luddite who sees no value in these electronic wonders, but they have a way of going overboard. The selling of Techno Dad as a guy who has found a way to successfully balance his family life with his professional life has spawned a raft of truly disgusting gimmicks for being a good dad without actually having to be present. Recently, I saw a magazine article that straight-facedly described a busy dad who had videotaped a personal good-night for his young son so that his wife (or possibly the child's nanny) could plug him in at nighty-night time. It is enough to make me nostalgic for a bumbling '50s dad.

And speaking of that bumbling guy, he has been cunningly recycled in the updated stereotype, *Mr. Mom.* Michael Keaton, in the movie of that title, set the tone for this stereotype role, which was then cloned in various TV series. In the film, the hero, a victim of corporate downsizing, finds himself unemployed and so his wife, played by Teri Garr, gets a job to support the family, leaving Keaton to take care of their three youngsters. At first, he is a first-class, slapstick bumbler, losing his kids in the supermarket, overflowing the washing machine, in general behaving like the classic '50s dunderhead whose powers of reason and common sense totally forsake him the moment he has to do anything around the house. In case we've missed the point, one of Keaton's wife's friends consoles him with, "You'll get it. Mommy training is very difficult."

But here's where the cosmetic update begins: Keaton becomes depressed trying to be Mr. Mom—he puts on weight, starts drinking beer at breakfast, gets hooked on soap operas. In short, he becomes a caricature of a lazy, empty-headed, stay-at-home mom. And so, in an effort to pull himself together, Keaton starts doing "man" things around the house like painting the fence, repairing the stairs, and, most significantly, relating to the kids less like a tender mom and more like a drill sergeant. Voilà, *Mr. Dad!*

At this point, I saw hints (albeit comic hints) of a significant Marathon Dad strategy: Keaton had realized that a dad is not a mom and was in the process of making the necessary adjustments. But this turned out to be just a tease, a winking bow in the direction of genuine enlightenment. In short order, Garr becomes a victim of sexual harassment by her boss and quits her job, and Keaton gets his job back. So, in the final scene, everything is back to "normal"—Dad working, Mom running the household. Of course, they are not the same people they were at the outset: they are wiser and more in touch with any number of laudable feelings.

This film, and the contemporary stereotype it endorses, are prime sources of confusion (and alibis) for men who seriously want to become successful Marathon Dads. For starters, the stereotype promotes the old idea of Dad as dunderhead around the house, laying the groundwork for that old-time alibi, "We're simply not naturally good at this kind of work—for us, changing a diaper is akin to rocket science." Next, it tickles that traditional marital tension born of the assumption that any woman who works is somehow at sexual risk, laying the groundwork for the kind of suspicion and resentment that make true cooperation between a man and his wife even more difficult. And most significantly, the film lulls us into thinking we can have things both ways without being hypocrites. In standard Hollywood fashion, Keaton gets to be both a traditionalist and an up-to-date kind of guy: after his stint as Mr. Mom, he can talk the talk of male enlightenment—especially talk about how important his family is to him—but he does not have to really walk the walk of a fully committed, sacrific-

ing father. This sets the stage for the kind of New Dad token-
ism that is rampant today: the father who talks about how
much he loves being with his children and who ceremoniously
makes them dinner, say, once a week, but who—hour for
hour—does not even come close to sharing the home workload with his wife.

9

The Final Hurdle

▼ ▼ ▼ ▼

Primal Fear—"I'm Going to Lose Everything I Ever Worked For"

Like a wanted criminal in a makeshift disguise, Marathon Dad is terrified that at any minute someone at work is going to find him out for the double-dealer he really is: *a man who has responsibilities and loyalties to his family as well as to his job*. And when Marathon Dad does get found out, he is sure that he will lose his job or, at the very least, his chance for advancement and a raise; he will lose the respect and trust of his co-workers; and finally, he will lose his identity as a professional.

Every moment on the job is colored by this fear. And Marathon Dad's reaction to this fear often has the ironic consequence of actually making him a less valuable worker. He feels guarded and withdrawn; he finds himself editing out mentions of his family in his office conversations for fear of calling attention to his other loyalty. He feels constantly watched and evaluated, which makes him nervous about his performance—and this nervousness, in turn, conveys the impression of a worker who lacks confidence. He is a worried man and so is joyless and defensive, therefore a lot less fun to be around and to work with. He looks depressed.

Every time this fearful working father says something like,

"I'd rather have the meeting on another day because Thursdays I pick up Joey at school," he can sense his professional stock dropping. He attributes every assignment that goes to someone else as a sign that his "divided loyalties" are costing him his career. When he is discussing home duties on the phone with his wife, he interprets every sidelong glance from his co-workers as a put-down.

Well, the sad truth is, it ain't all paranoia: some of Marathon Dad's fears are well founded. There really are bosses and co-workers out there who cannot accept the fact that some of us choose to be hands-on fathers as well as dedicated workers— and these are people who will try to make us pay a price for this choice. We will look into how to handle such people— and what our options are—in Part III, Politics.

But before we get to that point, we have to figure out if, indeed, our fears are real. Or are they merely products of our imagination? Because fears that have no basis in fact can only serve to make us unhappy, nervous, and, yes, less confident and less effective workers.

Marathon Dad's Fear Reality Check

Every day of his working life, Marathon Dad is presented with a series of if/then propositions: if I pick up Joey at school, I won't be able to attend the sales meeting; and if I don't attend the sales meeting and Ralph does, Ralph will probably get the Andersen account and I won't; and if I don't get the Andersen account, I probably won't get that raise or promotion. But are any of these if/then outcomes necessarily true? Are they even *probably* true? Check it out:

If I don't attend the sales meeting, how likely is it *really* that I will not get the Andersen account?

1. Is my boss going to be surprised that I'm not there, or did I discuss it with him beforehand and get his agreement that it was okay? Is there any way I could

have better communicated my family schedule to my boss?

2. If he agreed that it was okay for me to miss the meeting, do I have any reason to doubt his sincerity? Has he ever been hypocritical about such issues with me before?

3. Has he ever been hypercritical about such issues with any of my colleagues before?

4. Does my boss have a family and family responsibilities himself? Have we ever discussed the problems of juggling job and family with each other? (Or is it a subject I am afraid to broach with him? And if so, is this a legitimate fear?)

5. Is my performance at work first-rate despite my family responsibilities? Has it become less so since I assumed more family responsibilities? Or do I make up for any time lost on the job because of this with extra time/work on other occasions?

6. If my performance has remained at a high standard, do my boss and colleagues know that? If not, is there some way I can subtly make this known to those who count?

Now, let's return to the original question, **If I don't attend the sales meeting, how likely is it _really_ that I will not get the Andersen account?**

Very? Possibly? Not really very likely at all, now that I consider it coolly?

It often turns out that our fears are actually more the product of habitual guilt and insecurity than of the reality of our work situation. As many of the above Reality Check questions imply, many of our fears can be allayed—or at least clarified—by better, more open communication with our bosses and colleagues. (Much of Part III is devoted to learning how to initiate, frame, and maintain these on-the-job communications about our "other lives.")

PART II

PRACTICES

▼ ▼ ▼ ▼ ▼ ▼

Setting a Pace That Works with
Honest Priorities, Effective Time
Management, and Clear
Communications

10

It's About Time

▼ ▼ ▼ ▼

Okay, I can't ignore any longer that guy in the back row who's had his hand raised all through Part I—although I think I know what he's going to say:

"Terrific! We working fathers married to working wives need to get our heads on straight," he begins. "But all that's academic if we don't have the time to do what we want to, to do what we know we should do. *I know I don't have enough time!*"

Ah, but you do have enough time, my friend. We all do, although I'm not going to tell you that it's easy to grasp that fact or to use it. Far from it. Still, you are definitely right. *Time is what being a successful Marathon Dad is all about: finding it, using it wisely, mindfully, and effectively for everyone involved—your boss, your co-workers, your wife, your children, and, of course, yourself.*

To reach that point, we first need to get back into our heads for a moment to analyze how we think about time and what simple cognitive mistakes we may be making that keep us from having enough time to do everything that a successful Marathon Dad needs to do. From there, we can go on to analyze how we currently use our time, setting priorities, creating a new schedule that works, and, finally, communicating about time with everyone involved, including the basic business of negotiating tasks with the people around us.

The kinds of mistakes we often make when thinking about time tend to fall into one or both of two basic categories: 1) All time is the same (or an hour is an hour is an hour, no matter when or how we spend it or with whom); and 2) Everyone experiences time the same way I do.

All Time Is the Same (Not!)

The existentialists had it right when they made a distinction between "clock time," that objective ticking by of time out there, and "lived time," time as we personally experience it. Of course, you don't have to be Jean-Paul Sartre to figure out that an hour spent under the high-speed drill in the dentist's office goes by a whole lot slower than an hour stolen away in a saloon, drinking beer and watching a Celtics game. Still, we are prone to forget the distinction between clock time and lived time when we think about how we routinely spend time in our daily lives. And forgetting this distinction can lead us to divvying up our time in counterproductive, unsatisfying, and ultimately self-destructive ways. Let's start with a No-Brainer: **Some times of day are better for some tasks/activities than others.**

We all know that, for most of us, our brains tend to be sharper and better focused in the mornings than after lunch, and for this reason many of us make an effort to put our heavy-thinking tasks (say, writing a report) earlier in the working day than our light-thinking tasks (say, schmoozing with a client). But even though we are aware that not all of our hours are created equal in this respect, we tend not to give this fact enough weight in our daily scheduling.

One way we give it short shrift is by *not claiming* our time for its best period of use. For example, your wife suggests that you do the laundry (a task you've agreed to do) in the morning before you go to work, but you know you'd be better off getting to the office early and doing some hard-thinking stuff before the phone starts ringing, and saving the laundry for after supper, when your brain has slowed down. But instead of making this point to her, you shrug and do the laundry. Bad idea—at least in most of the cases I can imagine. The big question here is, *who owns your time?* You? Your wife? Your boss? We will get further into this later.

On the subject of Sharp-Brain Time vs. Slow-Brain Time, I should note that there are many tasks that we actually *do better* when our brains are beating only in three-quarter time. High on this list are many household tasks, such as laundry and dusting, and many child-care tasks, such as playing Parcheesi with a six-year-old. If we do the latter at our sharpest moments, we tend to be more impatient and more easily distracted and bored than if we are in slow-brain time; so, whenever possible, we should reserve these activities for slow-brain time. By the same token, at those late-in-the-day, slow-brain, and body-weary times, we should press ourselves to do these laid-back tasks even though we really would rather sack out on the couch. In general, we will be buying time that way, productive time for our sharper moments. And what is more, we may even be buying energy in this way: many a father has reported to me that lying on the rug, playing a mindless game of Parcheesi with his six-year-old, has turned out to be much more relaxing and restorative than lying on the couch with his head inevitably buzzing with all the worrisome mental flotsam and jetsam of the day.

The other major reason we do not schedule our lives so that we are doing tasks at their best-suited times is because we are stuck in unproductive, self-defeating habits of time use. I hate to admit it, but we, the male of the species, seem to have a special gift for falling into these time traps.

The Bad Habits of Guy Time

HABIT	BETTER USE OF TIME
We do what we like to do first.	Do what is time-of-day appropriate or what is most important first.
We do what we know how to do or are good at first.	Ditto.
We do the easiest things first.	Ditto.
We do the urgent before the important.	Ditto.
We do the most interesting thing before the necessary thing.	Ditto.
We wait until deadlines are upon us before we begin.	Ditto.
We do tasks that we can complete quickly first.	Ditto.
We do small jobs first.	Ditto.
We do jobs in the order in which they come to us.	Ditto.
We do what others (boss, wife, kids) want us to do first.	Ditto.

Short-term Time vs. Long-term Time

Virtually all of the above guy-time bad habits result from our current proclivity toward short-term time thinking as opposed to looking at our time and our lives and the lives of those around us from a long-term perspective. It's the American way, but it is often not the most personally satisfying or productive way. We are tuned to quick responses, quick results, quick profits. In part, this up-tempo ethos is the product of our techno-electronic age, an age in which we pull information off the Internet at the flick of a finger, an age in which beepers and cell phones and fax machines afford us instant communications (urging us to respond quickly, even if a more considered response would probably be better); in short, they create a Techno Dad who is quick to respond, but frequently from a distance. The mass media contribute to this breakneck rhythm, not just the two-second cuts of MTV, but the speed at which narratives unfold in TV and film dramas. (Compare the time it takes a relationship to develop in a 1940s film with how long it takes in a 1990s film.)

One way this up tempo plays out in Marathon Dad's life is what I have come to call the "Chaos Theory of Family Time." This refers to the growing tendency in many two-working-parent homes of always operating in high-speed, chaotic mode, a half-dozen activities going on at once, all of them attended and responded to by both parents. Conversations are in fragments ("Have you paid the garbage—-? No, 'pneumonia' begins with a *p*, Joey. . . . Somebody left the water running upstairs . . . Is the phone for me?"); every task is always half done, every motion gracelessly ambivalent, every relationship half fulfilled.

I have visited scores of families who operate continuously in this chaos mode, as well as having had hundreds of phone conversations with such families where Mom or Dad appears to be carrying on a conversation with one or more children while talking with me. These families claim that the incredible demands of so many tasks and so little time have forced them into this modus operandi. I am sympathetic to their plight (after all, the very term "Marathon Dad" suggests a kinetic, breathless MO, although the best runners know how to pace themselves and that, of course, is what we are really after here). But I suspect that these chaotic-time parents find something seductive in this accelerating family rhythm: always operating on quick responses gives them a buzz, like an air traffic controller or a member of SWAT. They feel heroic. Well, they really *are*, of course—all Marathon Dads and Super Moms are heroes in my book. But this chaos mode is counterproductive in the extreme. Our attention is forever divided, every task and person gets cheated. Often, both Dad and Mom get into this mode in tandem—it can become almost like a contest of who is more high-speed, shooting-from-the-hip than the other—and this makes the pattern even harder to break. But if this is the mode you find your family in, it is something you need to talk about and to break through together.

The "Chaos Theory of Family Time" is only the extreme case of short-term time overcoming our crowded lives. It invades us in subtler ways. To use the Techno Dad example again, the father who wears his beeper while playing catch with his son or daughter is sending his kid a disturbing message, namely, "I'm all yours until something really important comes up." This is not to say that there are not times when carrying a beeper can buy you time with your kids, time you wouldn't have available to them if you were tied to a phone or a desk; but when the beeper is always part of your standard uniform, part of who you normally are with your children, you are glued to short-term time at the cost of a long-term relationship.

Life's Timetables

The mistake mentioned above is the most salient point about short-term and long-term time. Our relationships with our wives and our children are long-term phenomena. Not only do they develop over the long haul, but each of them develop as individuals over the long haul. I have seen too many husbands and fathers who are perpetually playing "catch-up" with their children and wives. They are forever trying to make up for "lost time" with them, hoping they can quick fix things with an hour of play here or a dinner out there. Things don't work that way. Long-term relationships require long-term time thinking and scheduling. Each person in the family has his own image of who he is and where he is going, yet our tendency is to expect everyone to automatically conform to our own timetable. We also tend to assume that our children are at the level of development and autonomy that we expect, and not where they actually are in their lives. What many of us also forget is that our *careers* are long-term phenomena too. They have a trajectory and arc of their own that too often can become obscured by the exigent demands of the job.

In order to come up with a schedule that satisfies all of our main priorities, we need to start with this long view of things, a view that takes into account how our children change from year to year and how our career demands and goals change from year to year. For example, it is easy to see that in their first five months of life, our children need more of our time— or at least could greatly benefit from more time with us— than, say, during the last five months of their eighteenth year. But this principle applies across the board, from each child's birth to when he or she leaves home—and beyond. In short, during some periods of our kids' lives, they could use more time with us—and different kinds of time with us—than at other periods. Similarly, some periods of our careers—say the first six months on a new job—require more time and more dedication than others—say the final six months before retirement.

When we reflect on our priorities and when we set about making up our schedules, we should keep one eye cocked on these timetables.

Your Career

Where do you see yourself now? What "stage" of your career are you in? Early apprenticeship, learning? Established expertise and competency? Peak earning and production? Leadership, management, and autonomy? How much do you want to be earning at each stage of your career? What concrete accomplishments (e.g., design a freestanding building, sell $1 million in insurance, be named president of the company) do you hope to achieve by what age? These are all questions that you will want to weigh when you thoughtfully work out your priorities, but before you get to that point, take a stab at the big picture so that you will start working on those priorities with a sense of your entire career, not just what's due on your boss's desk next Tuesday.

YOUR LIFE STAGE	YOUR CAREER GOALS
Your current age _____	
Age in 10 years _____	
Age in 20 years _____	
Age in 30 years _____	
Age in 40 years _____	

Your Wife's Career

Where does she picture herself now and where does she picture herself in ten years? Twenty? Thirty? Clearly, there is only one definitive way to answer these questions—*ask her!*

HER LIFE STAGE	HER CAREER GOALS
Wife's current age _____	
Age in 10 years _____	
Age in 20 years _____	
Age in 30 years _____	
Age in 40 years _____	

Your Children's Development

What our children need and can gain at each stage of their lives can be defined in general terms:

Infancy: They do not necessarily need both parents simultaneously, but if there is to be genuine bonding with both parents, each of you has to spend a significant amount of time with the infant during those critical first six months.

Preschool: An age of high demand for teaching, play, language development, learning rules—all things that dads are naturally good at. (See "A Dad Is Not a Mom.")

School Age (Elementary): The kids have their first major contact with others for prolonged periods without their parents (if you did not use preschool). They need help learning how to communicate. Parents also have to provide a liaison with teachers and school officials. Traditionally, most of these contacts are Mom's, but this is an area where dads can help realign the gender imbalance found in most primary schools. (For example, dads who read stories to elementary-school classes are rare, but highly effective and appreciated, especially by the boys in the classroom.)

Junior High: Late latency period, the development of puberty. Father/son relationships are especially important here for modeling, counseling, and companionship. In many ways, your son's need for you now is as crucial as during the first six months of his life. Or, to put it another way, if you are not a genuine presence in his life at this stage, both of you may suffer consequences that are not easy to turn around later in his life.

High School: The push for greater autonomy and independence, hence the need for you to provide tolerant guidance and safe foundations so kids can "try out" adult behaviors (dating, working, driving—all key developmental milestones). In general, they'll need (and will want) a lot less face-time with you now, but still have to feel that you will be there when they really need you.

CHILD'S LIFE STAGE	YOUR ROLE WITH CHILD
Child's current age _____ Grade in school _____	
Age in 10 years _____ Grade in school _____	
Age in 20 years _____ School? Career? Marry? _____ _____	
Age in 30 years _____	
Age in 40 years _____	

Time Is the Same for All People (Not!)

To get this one, all we have to do is recall the way summer vacation seemed to stretch to infinity when we were school kids, and then compare that with how quickly a summer vacation flies by for us now. We experience the passage of time differently at different stages of our lives, and ignoring this fact can disturb our relationships, particularly with our children. Its immediate implication usually works in favor of our crowded schedules: an hour set aside for one-on-one face-time with our child will probably feel like a whole lot more to him or her, and that's just great.

But unfortunately, this fact has contributed to one of the most destructive myths of modern fathering and mothering: the Myth of Quality Time. The substance of this idea is that a brief amount of intense/fun-filled/highly involved and attentive time spent with a child is worth more than a much longer amount of casual/low-key/divided-attention time spent with a child. Obviously, there is some truth in this: if we are never fully focused on our child, always distracted or bored or heeding someone or something else, the child doesn't have a whole lot to relate to. But this is quite different from saying that brief but intense face-time *makes up for* extended, unhurried, yes, *casual* time spent with a child. This fallacious leap turns out to be more of a father's (or mother's) alibi for spending too little time with his child than a genuine principle for good fathering. *And our kids know it.*

I've spoken with a great number of children who told me that they have come to dread Quality Time. Here is what one frank, funny, and precocious ten-year-old girl had to say on the subject: "He [her father] lets me know around Monday that next Saturday we're going to do something special, just the two of us. I don't dare tell him that I want to play softball that day—you know, he'd be so disappointed and make me feel all guilty and everything. So I act like I can hardly wait. And then the big day comes and he's, like, so *ready*. Whatever we do, he looks at me so seriously, like he's expecting something from me—this great moment of bonding or something. I feel like saying, 'Give me a break,' but I don't. I just smile like I'm having the time of my life."

So much for Quality Time in that family.

A similar error can be made in our marital relationships. We set aside Two Quality Hours alone with our wives, and the time becomes so freighted with expectations of intimacy and/or sex and/or comfort that the stage is perfectly furnished for disappointment, sexual failure, and frustration. As the sages sang, "Can't hurry love."

Interestingly, the notion of Quality Time *does* have an application in the place where we probably least expect it: work. No matter how independent we may feel at the office, we are still often stuck with the mind-set of "putting in time" (or "doing time," as one hardworking friend of mine puts it): checking in and checking out at prescribed times each day, no matter how demanding or undemanding that particular day's tasks may be. Instead of organizing our workdays around what needs to get done and how long that will take, we inevitably find ourselves filling the day with whatever tasks need to be done,

big or small. But what if we were to take the idea of Quality
Time and apply it here? What if we were to look at a task or
a whole project in terms of how long it would take to get it
done if we dedicated a limited amount of intense/highly
involved and attentive time to it, as compared to the day-
in-and-day-out, low-key/divided-attention time we tend to
put into tasks across the board while we "do time" at work?
Such a switch in perspective has been known to lead many
a Marathon Dad to reconsider a formerly disdained idea
such as taking advantage of flex time or even paternity leave.
Short of that, the notion of Quality Time on the job can
serve as an important touchstone when we get down to the
business of creating an optimum Marathon Dad schedule.

Parallel Time vs. Multi-task Time

The primary reason that Quick Quality Time is a poor excuse
for fathering is that Long-Term Casual Time turns out to be
the stuff that good father-child relationships are basically
made of. When it comes to forging bonds, setting examples,
mentoring lessons, modeling roles, providing both a sense
of security and of authority, it is the no-frills, mundane
activities of eating meals together, driving to the dentist
together, watching TV together—*sitting in the same room
doing two different things together*—in which these basic
father-child transactions are most likely to occur. Yes, they
are most likely to occur over the long haul as compared
to during brief but intense, fun-filled/highly involved and
attentive Quality Time.

Lest this sound like "doing time" on the home front, let
me hasten to sing the praises of Parallel Time, which is basically the above-mentioned *sitting in the same room doing two
different things together*. You, say, are scanning business material you brought home in your briefcase or are reading the
paper, while Joey Jr. is doing his homework and playing with
his Gameboy. You are near enough to talk—from time to time,

Joey Jr. asks your input on a math problem; from time to time, you read aloud an item in the paper that you believe he will find interesting—but for the most part you are quiet, at ease, not intently focused on each other. In short, what is going on here is the diametric opposite of the model of Quality Time.

An obvious advantage of the Parallel Time scenario is that you have your cake and eat it too—guilt-free: You are getting some necessary task done (reading a report) and you are being a good dad at the same time. But there are other, less obvious advantages here as well. For one thing, parallel activity is less stressful on both of you: when time with your child is rare and "special," the high focus on the relationship is likely to give him or her the willies, as the ten-year-old girl so eloquently pointed out earlier. From your point of view, if you are stuck with the mind-set that you have to give your child absolute full attention whenever you are with her, you will probably find yourself avoiding her company when you simply want to read the paper or go over some reports. Furthermore, Parallel Time provides the optimum setting for that best father pedagogy of all: *modeling.* If you concentrate seriously on the report you are reviewing, Joey Jr. may very likely (consciously or unconsciously) take a cue from you and start focusing more seriously on his homework. If you are there to help him with his homework when he is stuck, but are not hovering over his shoulder waiting for him to come up with the right answers, he will better learn how to work on his own, yet he will do so with the security that help is at hand.

I must hasten to add that there is a fine but critical line between parallel activities and multitasking, which is the attempt to do two or more tasks simultaneously. If, say, your son needs *some sustained and concentrated* help with a homework assignment, any attempt to do some concentrated work on your own creates a lose/lose situation for both of you. He'll feel cheated and so will you. The difference between parallel activities and multitasking is a judgment call on a case-to-case basis, but the basic distinction to keep in mind is between alternating activities and doing them at the same time. A good way to monitor the difference is by watching your own reactions: if, say, you find yourself seriously annoyed when Joey Jr. distracts you from your report with a question about his homework, you know it's time to either put the report down for later or excuse yourself to another room.

Wasting Time and Finding Time

In the following chapter when we analyze exactly how we spend each hour of the day, we will undoubtedly turn up whole stretches of wasted time, time spent watching TV or on the Internet, for example. But perhaps the most adept "time thieves" in our lives are those bad habits listed at the outset of this chapter and these, in turn, tend to derive from some of the guilts, fears, and denials we examined in Part I. Dad guilt can create paralytic ambivalence ("I really should be doing my work instead of hanging out with my kids" / "I really should be hanging out with my kids instead of doing work."); Dad fear breeds Dad panic ("I'll never get everything done!"), which leads ineluctably to poor concentration and ill temper; Dad denial sets us up for broken promises and yet more Dad panic ("There will be plenty of time to help Joey Jr. with his homework after I finish revising this report"— even though there's no way in hell you'll be done with the report before midnight).

And so I say to the gentleman in the back row, getting our heads on straight is hardly academic when it comes to the business of making the most of our time as Marathon Dads. It is the necessary precondition for the nitty-gritty of creating a schedule that allows us to be dedicated, responsible workers *and* dedicated, hands-on fathers.

It's time to move on.

11

Who's on First?

▼ ▼ ▼ ▼

Establishing Honest Priorities

The first step is a leap of faith. **You have to decide that
establishing your priorities is your *first* priority. And
then you have to commit to doing so in a sustained,
thoughtful way.**

This means setting aside sufficient time in your schedule to
figure out what, ultimately, you value most in your life. Everything begins with this: a new schedule that works for you *and*
a position of certainty, security, and strength from which you
can discuss and negotiate time and tasks with everyone in your
life—your wife, your boss, your co-workers, and your kids.

Figuring out overall, long-term priorities is not something
that comes naturally to most of us. On the contrary, as we
race along Marathon Dad's cross-country course, we never
seem to have enough time to perform this cardinal exercise;
*we are too busy doing things to figure out why we are doing
them or even if we really want to do them.*

Indeed, on those rare occasions when we decide that it is
high time for us to step back and take stock of our lives,
we tend to become quickly distracted from this enterprise by
whatever demand or crisis presents itself: "I'll think about my
life later, but first I've got to get this report out . . . or pick

up the baby-sitter . . . or pay the bills." As Marathon Dads, we virtually always find ourselves in an environment crackling with stimuli—people who want things from us, deadlines that need to be met, tasks that must be done.

One husband and wife who came to me for counseling, Alex and Ginger, were so deeply embedded in their busy, daily routines that neither of them had taken a long view of their lives since they married, some seven-plus years earlier. Alex came from a long line of high achievers in investment banking, men who had gone from Princeton to Harvard Business School to Wall Street, and he was no exception to the family tradition, commuting each day from their sumptuous home in Connecticut to his office on "the Street." Ginger was a school administrator, already on the fast track to becoming principal of the local regional high school. They had three children whom they both adored. But something was missing when they sought my help, something neither of them could clarify.

I had a pretty good guess, the first time I saw them, about what was missing from their lives—*some regular, unhurried time together as a family*. But clearly, they had to come to this conclusion on their own, so I suggested that, *individually*, they take some time off to think about their priorities—what it is they each want most in their lives.

Both of them took my suggestion seriously and followed the guidelines for this task, which I will discuss shortly. When they returned for the next session, both were visibly excited by their discoveries. Ginger went first. Indeed, she had decided that what she wanted most was some *regular, unhurried time together as a family*. Bingo!

But it was Alex who blew my socks off. He took the idea of more family time to an unexpected level: "I realized that I've been living somebody else's idea of a good life," he began. "Like my father's idea . . . and his father's. But I don't like this life of being away from home and Ginger and the kids virtually all of the time. I don't like it. It's not what I want. It's not even close to my real priorities."

What Alex had realized that he really wanted was a job close to home, a job that allowed him to be home before dark every night of the week. "And I don't care how that reads in the Princeton alumni magazine," he said.

Changes were made. Needless to say, they found what was missing and then some.

Stepping outside the locus of day-to-day stimuli is a prime prerequisite for truly figuring out our priorities in a meaningful way. And, to come full circle, one of the *goals* of consciously establishing our priorities is to be free from being forever in a passive/responsive mode: always reactive and never proactive. And so to begin, we have to leap out of this circle of stimuli.

The Fine Art of Navel Gazing

No, I am not a practicing yogi or a Marist novitiate, but I do strongly believe that some fundamental endeavors in our lives require a still, neutral space in which to perform them—a retreat, if you will. Seriously establishing life priorities is definitely one of these endeavors. We cannot, for example, deliberate in a clear, unbiased fashion about what we ultimately value in our lives while seated in our office with the phone ringing or at home in the living room with the tube blaring and our family wandering in and out. For some of us, the ride between office and home may be a good place to start, although that tends to comprise too short a time for most of us to get sufficiently relaxed and distanced to look at our lives from the necessary grand, unhurried perspective. Some men have told me that they can achieve the proper frame of mind for basic stocktaking on long plane flights, a time in which they are literally neither here nor there. But for me, nothing beats a long, solitary hike in the woods, preferably lasting overnight: gone fishin'—for priorities.

Once the appropriate calm is achieved—a personal place devoid of routine demands and crises—throw a mental monkey wrench into the works: *imagine yourself in some extreme circumstance that totally changes your life.*

For example, imagine that your wife announces at breakfast one morning that she is leaving you and taking the kids with her. *What would you do? What would you miss the most? Regret the most? What would you wish you had done to prevent this moment from ever happening?*

Indeed, I am sure there are some of you reading this who have found yourself suddenly out of a marriage and family that you once believed would go on forever. If ever there was a time for rediscovering or re*designing* your priorities, this is it. Does the fact that you are now divorced mean that you value family life less than you did before? Not necessarily. You'll have to dig deep to find your own answer to this one.

The process of *establishing* priorities is, in fact, *discovering the priorities that you already have.* What an exercise like the one above does is bring your priorities to consciousness: it writes them large so you cannot miss them.

Here is another "as if" at the other end of the extenuating-circumstances spectrum: imagine that your boss calls you into his office and announces that you have been selected to take over his job as head of the company. *Would you accept on the spot? Would you request time to think it over? Okay—think it over! Is this offer really your fondest dream? What would you be willing to sacrifice to make this dream come true? Time with your family? Time with your friends?*

Again, your genuine priorities—possibly some that you have not been fully aware of before—will rise to the surface and present themselves for your conscious deliberation: *"Aha! So this is what I truly value."*

Some of you may be thinking that this exercise is ridiculously artificial and far too melodramatic. Be that as it may, in my experience and in the experience of scores of men whom I have counseled, these extreme-case scenarios provide a supremely clarifying lens through which to examine our lives. Yes, this technique borrows heavily from some of the cornier narratives in novels and movies in which some awful crisis befalls the hero, whereupon he has an epiphany about whom he really loves or what he really wants to do with his life, or worse, what he wishes he *had done* with his life but now it's too late. Very corny, yet in real life such circumstances vividly imagined can be wonderfully effective tools for elucidating our priorities. Because it turns out that for most of us, it takes imagining our lives in extremis to genuinely evaluate our day-to-day lives. *Defining Moments inform our most mundane moments.*

Here's another: imagine that the boss calls you into his or her office and tells you that you are fired, you've got thirty days left before you are cut loose without a life vest. *What is your first reaction? Anger? Panic? Perhaps relief? What would you do if you had to suddenly downsize your life considerably? What loss would hit you the hardest? What would you want desperately to maintain in your life under these new circumstances? What would you willingly give up? How do you think your wife and children would respond? What would this event do to your sense of self? Where would you seek comfort and solace?*

And again at the other extreme, here's an exercise that was originally designed for therapy with children, but which I have found particularly effective for adult men who wish to clarify their values: imagine what miracle could happen that would suddenly make everything in your life the way you want it. *A windfall of money? A new job? A new family? A full head of hair?*

Again, the exercise can free your consciousness to look at values that may be hidden from you behind the screen of stimuli in your busy, everyday life. Feel free, of course, to invent your own in extremis scenarios to shake out your priorities. I'll conclude this segment with the most devastating one on my list: **whom or what are you willing to die for?**

"What's that? Your children? You'd die for them in a heart-beat, you say? Well, then setting aside a couple of afternoons each week for them sure sounds like a small sacrifice to make—comparatively speaking, that is."

The preceding exercises free up your consciousness to consider all the legitimate contenders for your priorities. Now it's time to put them down on paper.

The List

As your priorities surface, jot them down. For now, don't attempt to put them in any order, just get them on paper. To begin with, most of us will come up with more or less the same list:

Family
Career
Wealth
Spiritual Development
Personal Development
Physical health
Community

It is a fine list, a good place to start, but it suffers from two major shortcomings: 1) It is so nonspecific that it is of little use in helping you decide where to put the emphasis—and dedicate the time—in your life; and 2) It is so inclusive that it makes virtually *everything* in your life a priority.

Two rules of thumb for composing your list follow from this:

1. Define your priorities as specifically as possible.
2. If everything is a priority, nothing is a priority, so ultimately you will have to do some fine-tuning, weighing one value against another until you have distilled your list to a genuine hierarchical rating of priorities.

Let's take a closer look at number 1. The priority "Family" can clearly be broken down into "Children," "Wife," and "Parents," but where do we go from there? For starters, consider the subcategory "Children" and ask yourself where, more precisely, your priorities lie here:

Is it most important for you to develop a good relationship with your children? To bond with them? To feel comfortable with them and them with you? To have fun with them? For them to respect you? Love you? Obey you?

Or is it most important for you to nurture your children into well-prepared, productive human beings? To teach them critical lessons for survival? For understanding the world and other people realistically? To teach them lessons for personal advancement? For being good students? For getting the most out of life?

Or is it most important for you to develop your children's values? To provide them with idealism? With a spiritual life? With a clear sense of right and wrong? To set an example for them?

Clearly, the implied values in your answers to these questions can easily overlap; for example, developing a good relationship with your children has obvious implications for teaching them all kinds of lessons. But your goal here is to focus on basics—what comes first—not on what follows from these basics. As well, it is obvious that the questions I have offered above are just the beginning of what may very well be a much longer list of questions for you to ask yourself about what specifically you want to happen between yourself and your children. It is up to you to ferret out those additional questions and your answers to them. And then, of course, you must write them down.

How do you go about breaking down the values you have invested in your wife and marriage?

How important to you is the companionship of your wife? Sex with her? Love? How important is marital security and

*solace? Is a successful working partnership with her enough
for you now? Forever?*

And here are a few questions you might ask yourself to help
you clarify your values in "Career":

*What is your primary goal in your career? Status? Power?
Wealth? If it is status, in whose eyes? Your peers'? Your
wife's? Your parents'? Your kids'? Your own? Do you have
clear and considered career expectations over the long haul,
say, where you want to be by the time you are thirty? Forty?
Fifty? How will it affect you if you do not achieve these in-
terim goals? If you do not achieve your long-term goals? How
much do you want to stake of your sense of self and your
sense of self-worth on achieving these goals?*

*If wealth is your goal, how much? By when? What do you
want to do with your money? How much do you need to feel
secure? To feel that you have everything you really need?
How much beyond that is important to you?*

Remember, values will not necessarily translate into those
things that you like to do or are good at or which other people
expect you (or a man like you) to do. To take what seems to
be my favorite example, you may not like changing diapers or
even be good at it, but you may put a high value on being a
fair father/partner (a moral value) or you may view diaper
changing as a highly important activity for bonding early with
your child. If either of these latter suggestions is true for you,
that means you value diaper changing, like it or not.

I have now suggested enough questions for you to continue
on your own in all of your major categories. Give yourself lots
of time and a whole notebook's worth of paper.

The Ratings Game

Now that you have listed, as specifically as possible, what it is
you value, it is time to turn to number 2, narrowing down
and rating these values; in short, creating genuine, *usable*
priorities.

To get yourself started, run through your list and check off those values that are indisputably less than contenders for top priority. In practical terms, these are the items you can live without, or at least live without devoting a significant amount of time to them. On my personal hit list, "getting filthy rich," "developing a killer physique," "hanging out regularly with my buddies," and "learning French" bit the dust at this stage.

Now take a second pass at your list, asking yourself, "If I had to cut down this list to only five or six items, what could go?" The operative principle here is *not* that the newly subtracted items will be de facto totally eliminated from your life, *just that they will be eliminated from your top priorities*. What you want to end up with is a list of five or six items that define your major overall goals for the next chunk of your life. In a sense, this list defines the man you want to be.

Such a list should be able to fit (in your personal shorthand) on the back of a business card. I mean that literally. Write down the items on a business card and stick it in your wallet. You will be referring to these values frequently as you create a new schedule that embodies them. You may also want to sneak a glance at them from time to time when critical either/or propositions present themselves to you at work or at home.

One final thought here: I find it helpful to set time aside twice a year (or whenever you are starting to feel particularly overwhelmed or confused) for a close inspection and possible revision of my priorities. Our circumstances change with time, as do our values and our selves. As we have observed already in examining our Family and Career timetables, what is a priority now may not be one later on, and vice versa. A man has to keep up-to-date with himself.

In Dreams Begin Responsibilities: Translating Priorities into Time

In the last analysis, discovering and establishing your priorities is an act of claiming ownership of your time: *"This is what I personally want to do with my life, and time is the substance of my life.*" From this claim follows your responsibility *to yourself* to have your schedule reflect those things that you really value in your life.

At the outset of this book, we looked at an overview of what appears to be the Irreconcilable Differences between the values we invest in our professional lives and those we invest in our family lives. I said then that I do not believe these differences have to be mutually exclusive and I stand by that assertion. But now we are getting down to the nitty-gritty of sorting out the hours of our days and weeks so that they translate our values into actions, and this is a far-from-easy or self-evident task.

No matter how finely we try to tune our priorities, they remain abstractions until we translate them into specific time use. If, say, we have determined that we put a high priority on teaching our children critical lessons for survival, what activities and tasks with our kids should we earmark in our weekly schedules? Going on hiking trips? Bringing them to our office from time to time to see the work we do? Reading them stories that teach the lessons we want to pass on?

And if, say, we have placed a high priority on maintaining an ongoing sexual relationship with our wife, what does this mean about scheduling time with her? That we should actually schedule sex with her? (I think so, but more about that later.)

And if we put a high value on fairness in our marital relationship, does this mean we should aim for an equitable distribution of home and child-care tasks with our wife? (I think this is inevitably so, but again, more on this later.)

As we proceed with the task of translating priorities into time use, keep in mind that by narrowing down our priorities, we have gained some flexibility and, in fact, we have gained some time by eliminating those areas where we do not truly want to spend (or waste) our time. In short, this step is not simply a question of either/or, as in "*Either* I spend time developing my relationship with my children *or* I spend time advancing my status in the firm." Rather, it is a question of *finding a balance of time that works for all of your top priorities.*

12

"Did I Really Do That?"

▼ ▼ ▼ ▼

Analyzing Your Time

Here is a sure way *not* to figure out how you are currently using your time: *sit in a quiet room with a notebook and approximate from memory just how much of your time you spend on your job, with your kids, with your wife, doing household tasks, commuting, at recreation, etc.*

Judging by my results and those of others who have tried this technique, your answers will be off the mark somewhere in the area of fifty percent. Nice try (usually, a nice *self-serving* try), but this method of time analysis does not provide the kind of hard information we are going to need to construct a workable new schedule for Marathon Dad. The only legitimate way to gather that information is the old-fashioned way: *keeping a careful time log in a date book.* Your best bet is to note down your activities for *every fifteen-minute interval for the whole twenty-four hours of every day for a minimum of two weeks (four weeks is better).* This should definitely include weekends too.

Here are a few entries from mine, by way of example:

DAY/TIME:	Monday/A.M.
6:15	wake/Elena
6:30–7:00	coffee/paper
7:00–7:30	lunches/bus
7:30–8:30	Owen/prep/drive to school
8:30–9:00	commute to office
9:00–10:30	team mtg.
10:30–12:00	clinical sessions
(and so on)	

Even using this method, we have to guard against cheating—say, shading fifteen minutes here or there over into the kids' column because it just "feels right." One specific I would urge you to be particularly honest about is those clips of time when you are doing neither one thing nor another, but attempting to do two or more things or waiting to do something. Another caveat: be sure to note all the time you spend alone with your wife and *exactly what you do in that time,* be it watching TV or making love. Hey, nobody else needs to see this personal-time breakdown, and an honest analysis of how much time you spend with your wife can be one hell of a wake-up call.

Once we've got the facts of how we spend our time down in black and white, we need to ask ourselves Five Fundamental Questions about each time entry:

1. Does this item correspond to one of my top priorities? Obviously, some entries will not correspond to your priorities but are there for what appear to be necessary, pragmatic reasons—for example, "commuting." Others will scream out at you: *"Hey, I'm only doing this out of habit, not because I really value it!"* Still others will only whisper that they do not match up with your primary values because there is some real ambiguity there. Listen to these most carefully.

Our biggest hurdle here is *translating particular priorities into specific tasks,* and vice versa. If, say, we have concluded that, above all, we value a good relationship with our children, one that emphasizes openness and affection, we may very well decide that the time we spend helping Colin with his math homework is not as on target prioritywise as, say, going to the airport with him every Sunday afternoon. This does not mean, of course, that we cannot do both and then some. But the basic point of this exercise is to pinpoint those items we really need to spend time on—perhaps, *much more* time on—and which items we are willing to let go in order to gain time for those things we value more. Both the above-mentioned "screams" and "whispers" items will become prime candidates for the old heave-ho when you create your new schedule.

2. Which items that appear to be pragmatically necessary would I feel okay about having someone else do? I am referring here to such tasks as, for example, driving my son to school. On the one hand, this way of spending time with him may perfectly correspond to one of my "Children" priorities; but on the other, it may not—and dropping it from my schedule may allow me to do something else with my boy that I value more.

When I suggest that there may be some activities or tasks that you feel okay about leaving for someone else to do, I want you to consider this prospect somewhat abstractly and without prejudice. Perhaps there are some tasks or activities that you would feel comfortable about having only your wife or your father-in-law do in your place. Whatever; that is not your concern here. Just note those things that you would willingly relinquish from your own schedule; we will worry about who will do them in your stead later on.

Likewise, do not concern yourself with whether or not any particular outsourcing service exists at your place of work or in your community before you decide that such and such a task is one that you would willingly pass up to give you more time for something else. Suffice it to say here that one of our main objectives in Part III will be to discover how to *create* new outsource services for yourself and other Marathon Dads.

3. Which items in your existing schedule are time-wasters for other reasons? To get a handle on this one, all you have to do is refer back two chapters to the infamous "Bad Habits of Guy Time." Check each item of your time use against each one of these sneaky time-wasters. The results of this little exercise, done with brutal honesty, can be a real eye-opener. Hours of newly found time will suddenly manifest themselves to the vigilant.

4. Which items have become a part of my schedule without my ever having consciously planned for them to be there? Obviously, some items which have become part of our routine without our having consciously put them there are nonetheless activities or tasks that actually do reflect our priorities. But if these items got there on their own—probably because someone else plopped them there—you need to consider them thoughtfully now. The easiest way for someone else's priorities to sneak into your schedule is for you to not have yours established solidly in the first place.

5. Which individual items or overall distribution of items strike me as patently unfair in terms of the breakdown of tasks between me and my wife? Between me and my co-workers? Needless to say, this one is a biggie, one that has a great deal riding on it in many areas of your life. Clearly, you cannot do a final fair-time analysis until you communicate and negotiate with your wife and your co-workers, a communication that will necessarily include their own analysis of the hours of their days. We will get into that in the next chapter. But before we reach that point, we need to make some tentative judgments about fair distribution of tasks, some educated guesses. These judgments should take into account 1) your personal priorities; 2) a principle of equal time *or* equal work (some tasks take longer but are easier, and vice versa); and 3) the Principle of Complementarity that we explored in Part I (we are better suited to/more appropriate for some tasks than our wives are, and vice versa).

The Last Analysis

None of these Five Fundamental Questions is easy to answer, particularly not the first. But answer them we must, thoughtfully, honestly, and without further delay. And we must keep careful track of our answers. To do this, add five columns to your time log.

DAY/TIME	1. Priority?	2. Outsource?	3. Waste?	4. Planned?	5. Fair?
Monday					
6:15 wake/ Elena					
6:30–7:00 coffee/ paper					
7:00–7:30 lunches/ bus					
7:30–8:30 Owen/ prep/drive to school					
8:30–9:00 commute to office					
9:00–10:30 team mtg.					

   Make your responses in each column as concise and definitive as possible; in most cases, a simple "Yes" or "No" should do the trick. Do not get lazy and do not get sloppy: this annotated time log is going to be your bible as you move on to creating a balanced schedule that works for you.

13

A Well-Balanced Life

▼ ▼ ▼ ▼

Creating a Marathon Dad Schedule That Works

W e have thought through our priorities and we have analyzed how we currently spend our time. Now we are ready to take the plunge and reconstruct our schedules so that the Irreconcilable Differences that stared us in the face at the beginning of this venture can be reconciled in a schedule that balances our desire to be first-rate fathers with our desire to be first-rate professionals.

But first I need to respond to those groans and titters I hear in the back row. I know what you guys are thinking: *"Sure, John, I can construct perfect schedules until I'm blue in the face. But it's an exercise in futility, for all the good these schedules will do me in* real *life!"* What this man means, of course, is that his life is too chaotic, too subject to other people's demands, too unpredictable, to ever fit into some well-thought-out schedule.

My response is twofold. On the one hand, living a chaotic life that is forever responding to whatever task or personal demand presents itself *is the very reason you need to create a schedule—and to try valiantly to stick to that schedule.* Because what is missing in your life is *control over your time;* without control, you cannot begin to satisfy any of your priorities, either at home or at work. Constructing a schedule that works is the primary way that Marathon Dad takes back the control of his life that he has let slip away through thoughtlessness, weakness, conformity to stereotypes, fear of recriminations, avoidance of guilt, or any other of the host of emotional demands and cognitive confusions that tend to beset us. In short, creating a schedule is the first step in taking back our time, *and owning it.*

On the other hand, I am not about to argue that we can control *everything* in our lives or *all* of our time—that is simply not possible for men with the complicated lives that we have. But what we *can* do is be well prepared for the contingencies that regularly crop up in our lives—say, a sick child or the sudden need for trouble-shooting on an out-of-town project. We can have contingency plans and support systems that are in place, ready to be called upon when the occasion demands. I will address these in detail later in this chapter.

And there is something else we can do at this point, something as important as contingency planning, if subtler to execute. *We can maintain consciousness of our priorities so that when surprising circumstances or sudden demands arise, we have a mental matrix in place for deciding how—or even if— to handle them.* Let me harken back to what I said at the outset of this book, about reconciling our primary allegiance to Fatherhood with our primary allegiance to Career: "*We think through and establish a checklist of priorities—maxims for choices that we can feel comfortable with and confident in . . . Once we establish clear priorities, we will behave consistently.*"

Okay, let's get back to creating that schedule.

The Cardinal Rule: Use the Same Date Book for both Work and Home

When you think about it, this one is a no-brainer, yet most of us persist in keeping one agenda book for work and one (if any) for our home and fathering responsibilities. Implicit in such an arrangement is the idea that our business agenda book is the *real* one, the one that always takes precedence over any other responsibilities or events.

Keeping one agenda for both work and home responsibilities forces you to confront your intentions and priorities concretely. For example, for most of us it is "natural" to plan far-off work responsibilities as soon as we become aware of them; a conference in Toledo two months hence goes right into our agenda book. But we tend *not* to plan far-off family events in the same way. Somehow Emily's dance recital tomorrow comes as a total surprise, although we heard about it weeks— possibly even months—ago. But we did not note it in our schedule, at least not in the same date book in which we marked down that Toledo trip the moment the boss told us about it. Suffice it to say that if you find yourself deciding whether or not to go to Emily's recital the day before it is to happen, you are undoubtedly doing something wrong, something you need to correct now. This does not mean, of course, that you necessarily should decide to attend the recital, just that you have to keep track of family events as methodically as work events. Not to do so is a way of being dishonest with yourself and with your family; it provides you with a phony excuse for bowing out of family events ("Geez, I'd love to go to your recital, honey, but I've got this meeting I promised to go to").

So, ancillary to the rule of One Agenda Book for All Events is the rule to Note and Plan All Family Events As Far Ahead As Possible. We tend to reserve long-term planning for our jobs while we tend to fly by the seat of our pants—dealing with events on a day-by-day basis—when it comes to our families. Not right. Let's change that now.

Hidden Time Need #1: Transitioning

In our well-warranted enthusiasm for creating a tight, efficient, and priority-satisfying new schedule, we may overlook some important hidden time needs. High on this list is the need of Periods of Transition—time set aside for the express purpose of shifting psychological and metabolic gears as we go from work to home and, possibly, from home to work. Without the time and intent to make this a smooth transition, we can end up with what I call (only half jokingly) Marathon Dad Multiple Personality Disorder. A sufferer of this disorder has been known to walk in his front door in mid-sentence of an argument he is having in his head with a co-worker and thus be distracted and remote when wife or kid greets him—or worse, be gruff and argumentative with them. I am always reminded of those old "Blondie" comic strips in which Dagwood is yelled at by his boss (Mr. Dithers), comes home, and barks at his wife, who screams at her kids, who kick the dog (Daisy).

Another way this disorder manifests itself is in inappropriate styles of communication, especially with children. In this scenario, the man who returns home with his office life still ricocheting off the walls of his cranium, starts talking to his wife or children using the same vocabulary and *with the same attitudes* that he uses on the job. This situation is subtler to spot in yourself, but if you find yourself getting puzzled and/or annoyed looks from wife or child after you've exchanged a few words at the dinner table, the chances are you are a victim of this transition confusion.

One way to deal with this confusion is to attempt to become more conscious of how the culture of your workplace insinuates itself into your head. Every once in a while, try being a fly on the wall of your office and watch the way you interact with your co-workers, clients, and superiors. The point is not to "see through" yourself as some kind of phony persona, but to see what aspects of your personality are brought out by and are appropriate to your work situation. If being blunt and direct does the job on the job, all well and good; and if being hail-fellow does you well in some work situations, terrific. Simply be aware that these persona have their place, and that place, most of the time, is *not* around the family dinner table.

But the basic way to deal with Marathon Dad Multiple Personality Disorder is simply to *earmark time for transition* between work and home (and vice versa, if necessary). Obviously, the best time and place to do this is during your commute. And in my experience, the best way to use this transition time is to occupy yourself with some *third thing* that is neither work- nor home-related, say reading the newspaper or a piece of fiction, taking a nap, meditating, or listening to music. In this manner you empty your head of the goings-on of whence you've come and arrive in your new surroundings fresh and attentive to who and what await you there. Again, this may strike many of you as a no-brainer, but all I have to do is traipse down the aisles of any commuter train or bus and see all those open briefcases and laptop computers to realize that this is a no-brainer that few men are heeding. Of course, those briefcases and laptops are all open in the name of *time efficiency*—cramming every minute with tasks to be done so that there will be a net gain of time to do other things, say hang out with the family.

But this strategy often fails for one (or both) of two reasons. First, most of these men on the train bent over their file folders and reports never do get around to using their net-gain time for their nonwork-related priorities; more than likely, they are workaholics who fill *whatever* time they have with their professional work. And second, even if they do intend to dedicate their gained time to hanging out with the family, their heads will undoubtedly lag far behind their bodies as they walk in the front door. The net result will be *clock time* spent with their family that is sadly devoid of *lived time*. In short, they'll be there in body but will be absent in spirit, and so would have been far ahead of the game if they had set aside some transition time.

As a rule of thumb, I suggest setting aside a minimum of *fifteen minutes* for transitioning between work and home (most men tell me they need less or even zero transition time going in the other direction). I know that many of you will resist consciously dedicating time to transition: you feel instinctively that it is a waste of time and, further, that you have the self-control to transition on a dime, so the idea does not apply to you. My guess is that you are wrong. At the very least, give it a try: *Put fifteen minutes of transition time on your new schedule now.* It will become a useful habit before you know it.

Hidden Time Need #2: Rest and Recreation

Super Mom's first clue that having it all wasn't going to be easy came when she found herself dropping off to sleep in her child's bed every night while she read him his bedtime story. She already gave her all at the office, and now the Exhaustion Factor was kicking in. The inevitable result of chronic fatigue which follows from chronic overwork is *mediocre performance on both fronts, home and work.* Fatigue sets the stage for poor judgment, slow and inappropriate reactions, simple mistakes, impatience, and a foul temper. This was a painful lesson for Super Mom, one that demanded a critical reappraisal of her life and her schedule. Above all, those mid-bedtime-story collapses were what led her to help establish such workplace innovations as on-site child care and job-sharing. They also led her to find or create new outsources of home and child-rearing duties. And finally, this lesson prompted her to request a more equitable distribution of household and child-rearing tasks between Working Mom and her co-worker, Working Dad.

We men have a harder time admitting to fatigue. It just isn't manly to poop out—or at least, to recognize and concede to pooping out (it's the old Wimp Factor again). But trying to put in a full day's professional work *and* a full day's housework and child care *is* exhausting. And whether we like to admit it or not, we pay a price for it in our performance, not to mention in our health.

One way we pay that price is in virtually always being tired when we are with our children. It is only natural: at least five days of the week we see them mainly at the end of the day, after we've put in a hard day's work, possibly even after we've had a major workout at the gym. Along with this end-of-the-day fatigue come the usual symptoms: impatience, irritability, distractibility. What too often happens is that this End-of-the-Day Dad becomes the *only* dad our kids really know; they come to think of us as always being this way—that is, tired, impatient, irritable, and distracted. Not only do our children (not to mention our wives) get cheated this way, but we cheat ourselves out of some wide-awake, fully engaged, and focused time with our children—time when we can enjoy their company to the fullest. Granted, earlier on I extolled the virtues of being only half awake for *some* activities with our kids, but the question, as always, is one of balance. And what most of us need to schedule in order to maintain that balance is more Wide-Awake Time with our children.

The obvious place to begin is to plan Wide-Awake Time with our families on weekends, especially when our children are young (teenagers tend not to have much time for *us* on weekends). *What? You say you'd rather be fresh and wide awake for your golf game? Take another look at that business card with your priorities listed on the back and we'll discuss this again.*

The next place to look for Wide-Awake Time with your children or your wife is in your mornings, before you go to work. If the existing time demands of your job allow, you may want to drive or walk your children to school, wide awake and ready and willing to talk with them. (If the existing time demands of your job do not allow for this lovely interlude with your kids, you may want to see what can be done about restructuring your work schedule to provide for it; more about this option in Part III.) Or perhaps this morning walk with the kids is an activity you would like to do alternately with your wife.

Another option worth considering is getting up an hour or so earlier than is needed to merely have breakfast and be at work on time. Again, this is Wide-Awake Time that you can use for child care (if the kids are up) or, my favorite, for some high-quality time with your wife. We'll get further into this soon, but for most Marathon Dads and Super Moms, nothing can be sweeter after all those nights of "I'm too tired, dear" than some *untired* and *unhurried* morning lovemaking.

Now we arrive at a more complicated option: afternoons, when normally you would be at work. When your children are young, there will inevitably be some occasions when either you or your wife will need to dedicate some afternoon time to your children—getting them to a doctor's appointment or picking them up at school. To be sure, both of these examples could be dealt with by outsources, but there will always be exceptions when these sources are unavailable. And what is more, most of us do not want to *always* have our kids in the hands of surrogates. Freeing up afternoon time, either on a regular or an exceptional basis, requires negotiations with your employer and co-workers, dicey but necessary stuff that we will explore in Part III. My main point here is that before you consider whether or not you want to approach your employer and co-workers with some kind of time-off-in-the-afternoon proposal, ask yourself how valuable such an option would be for you in terms of *your priorities, the Fresh Time/Tired Time balance of your schedule*, and *the equitable distribution of tasks and time with your wife*.

So now we have another important principle to utilize in creating a workable Marathon Dad schedule: *create a schedule that realistically takes into account the Exhaustion Factor*. Balance is the key and here's where the metaphor of "Marathon" Dad fits the best: a good marathon runner knows how to pace himself, when to husband his energy and when to let it rip. The same goes for Marathon Dads: pace yourself. For example, let's go back to that workday problem of arriving home from the office too tired to really be there for your wife or kids. Could you work things out so that between work and home you do something that renews your energy—such as take a nap, meditate, or listen to some soothing music? By pacing yourself that way, you may be able to buy yourself some Wide-Awake Time with your family when you arrive home rested. And perhaps that after-work workout in the gym really is not scheduled optimally for good pacing; maybe a lunch-hour workout would provide better balance. And here's a radical idea that has worked for scores of men I know: combine your physical exercise time with family time. Perhaps go jogging with your infant in one of those jogging strollers, or go bicycling with your ten-year-old. Or plan regular evening swims with your wife—remember, baby-sitters are not only for dinner and movie nights.

Finally, when you start filling in your new schedule, *do not include more than you can honestly do without being perennially exhausted.*

Hidden Time Need #3: Sex and Marriage

When you were twenty and your top hormonal and emotional priority was sex, you could always find time to squeeze this pastime in, as it were. And you would have laughed if someone had told you that some years hence, when you were deep into your career and raising a family, this priority would slip so far down in your crowded schedule that sexless days would stretch into sexless weeks and then some. Well, gentlemen, this is no laughing matter for many of us these days. One of the biggest casualties of Marathon Dad's and Super Mom's demanding schedules is time alone together, most particularly sexual time.

I have one piece of sage advice here: *schedule it!*

Yes, I know that nothing sounds quite so unromantic as planning time for sex, but believe me, it is far better than the alternative, which is relatively little (or zero) time for sex.

Furthermore, scheduling sex does not have to preclude spontaneous sexual encounters with your wife; it simply means that you are not leaving your entire sexual fate up to these spontaneous encounters that have a way of disappearing under the strains of time pressures. And as one of my patients aptly put it, "Once we get started, it doesn't matter whether we planned it or we came running across a crowded room and fell into each other's arms—it's still sex and it's still good."

Finding private, undisturbed time for sex when our children were young was problematic even before both parents were working. Anyone who has had coitus interrupted by a knock on the door and a small voice crying, "I had a bad dream," knows what I am talking about. But now that we are both working, finding private time alone with our wives is especially troublesome because somehow it often feels that this time seems like time stolen away from being with our children— and we already feel that we are cheating our children on that score. The question is, of course, why should time alone with our wives feel any more like time stolen from our kids than, say, time at the office? And the answer appears to be a low-level confusion that many of us fall into: because our wives and our kids live in the same place, namely home, the mere logistic option of having both of them near makes us feel that time with one is time taken away from the other.

Happily, this confusion does lead to a novel and very rational solution to the problem, a solution I recommend to many couples: *not only schedule sexual time together, but schedule it for* someplace outside the house—*say a hotel or motel room.* As well as removing you from the scene of those nocturnal knocks on the door, this maneuver provides a far more romantic setting than a toy-strewn bedroom, more than compensating for the lack of romance implicit in scheduled sex. The planning for such an event is remarkably simple: you get a baby-sitter, just like you would if you were going out to the movies—but instead of going to the movies, you check into a motel. And although you may leave an emergency number with the sitter, no one has to have any idea what your evening's entertainment is.

Obviously, time for sex is not the only time you should schedule for your wife and yourself alone. An evening at the movies, ballroom dancing, playing indoor tennis—whatever your mutual fancy is—*also belong in your date book on a regular basis*. Believe me, if you do not schedule these things, they just do not happen. And if they do not happen with any regularity, the strain will start to appear in your marriage. I have seen too many working couples become finely meshed co-workers on the home front, only to discover that they have all but forgotten how to mesh on the romantic/sexual front. This is not good for anyone involved, even, ultimately, the children, who intuitively know when their parents are not really enjoying each other and suffer subtle emotional harm because of it.

One final thought here: as always, the time we set aside for one part of our lives has to be subtracted from time in some other part of our lives, and this, of course, goes for the time we set aside for being alone with our wives. I have always found that a prime candidate for time to "subtract from" is the time we spend as a couple at social events, especially those that have the ineluctable feel of social obligations. Honestly, what would you rather do, spend an evening alone with your wife in a motel room, or spend an evening with your wife at the Livingstons' dinner party? *It's time to whip out your list of priorities again.*

Found Time: Outsourcing

When it comes to household helpmates and child-care surrogates, Super Mom has again led the way. It started with a weekly housecleaner and was followed quickly by a preschool-age child-care service and/or an after-school child-care service. Then came laundry services, call-in grocery shopping services, taxiing services for regular private lessons and for irregular dentist and doctor appointments. Tutors to help the children with homework came next, then an expanded menu of after-school lessons and activities to occupy the children during working hours—karate lessons, tap-dance lessons, photography lessons, macramé lessons, you name it.

Some of this help came via pooling tasks (such as taxiing the kids) with other parents or farming them out to grandparents and friends, but most of the outsourcing of home and child-care tasks went to private individuals and /commercial agencies. It was the free-market economy operating at its most efficient: a need for helpers and surrogates begat a veritable cottage industry of services to meet specific requirements.

At first, the basic calculus by which Super Mom determined whether or not she would avail herself of a particular out-source was by looking at the rate of exchange. *Did her own hourly wage cover the cost of child care?* If it did not, she might have decided to cut back to part-time work. But later on, as it became clearer to most women that the reason they were working was not merely to post a net gain of money, but also to expand their horizons outside the home—to develop a identity that transcended that of just housewife—this calculus alone no longer did the trick. Now it became sufficient to simply *break even* by working and hiring a surrogate to fill in on the home front; and sometimes it was even worth it to post a small loss to maintain her career.

Only later did a new consideration enter the picture. *With all these surrogates, were the kids missing out on something fundamental in their relationship with their parents?* The answer to this question led to a much more complicated calculus for deciding which outsources were desirable and which were not, a calculus that took into account the effects of all these services on our children and on our basic sense of what a family should be.

It was at about this point that we, the Marathon Dads, came on the scene, ready to play a greater role in our home and family lives. A whole raft of home and child-care outsource services was already in place for us to choose from. Further-more, the model and mechanisms for creating new such ser-vices had already been established by our working wives. All well and good: *outsourcing* is *a primary way we can gain time to dedicate to higher priorities.*

But truth to tell, it was the price many of us fathers saw our children paying as a result of spending so much of their time with people other than their parents that prompted some of us to decide that we wanted to participate more fully in the upbringing of our children. Something wasn't working and we knew we were the key to fixing it.

First, we recognized that the reason our wives were em-ploying all these services for household and child care was because we were not contributing anywhere near enough in these areas. So many of us began looking for ways where we could replace the surrogates. *"Hey, why should we have a tutor helping Joey with his math homework? I can do that!"* Few wives would argue with that decision on our part, as long as we really did make it a regular part of our schedule and not another hit-or-miss dad phenomenon.

In short, the surrogates and other outsources that our wife might already have put into place to make her life manageable forced us to reconsider where we ourselves wanted to be re-placed by surrogates and where we did not. It was no longer an option to say to our wives, *"I don't think Joey is getting enough face-time with his parents in this new setup, so I want you to take him to soccer practice."* Nope, it was put-up or shut-up time. If we were not willing to take up the slack ourselves, we had forfeited our right to complain about who *was* taking up the slack.

Well, almost. I believe that it is still perfectly reasonable for us to say to our wives that we do not like or approve of a particular surrogate and therefore would like to find another. This position, of course, obligates us to find a suitable substi-tute ourselves. I think it is also reasonable for us to call for a family powwow to discuss the whole business of which home and family tasks you *both* feel good about farming out and which you do not. (More about this later under "Time Negotiations at Home.")

But the question remains of how you yourself make the decision of where you want to use outsourcing and where you do not. Here is where our priorities come in again. Let us say, for example, that you have determined, in the grand scheme of your relationship with your children, that having a close and comfortable relationship with them takes precedence over their being first-rate students or having "proper" respect for you and your abilities. (Again, I know these goals are not mutually exclusive, but we are talking about where we want to put your prime emphasis as a father.) In this scenario, you may well decide that hiring a tutor to help your son with his math homework is fine with you; it frees up other time you may want to spend with your boy, perhaps driving him to soccer practice or going clothes shopping. In fact, it may even strike you that tutoring your own son in math might create some friction and discomfort between the two of you that you would both be better off without.

I have discovered one general priority that seems to cut across the entire issue of outsourcing for virtually every man I have spoken with, and it translates into this general maxim: *whenever you can, choose household outsources over child-care outsources.*

The reason for this is obvious: in terms of our relationships, nothing is lost by having a hired hand mow the lawn or clean the house or do the shopping, but much can be lost if we have a hired hand take care of our children in whatever capacity. Clearly, this does *not* mean that we should dispense with *all* child-care surrogates; without preschool, for example, it would probably be impossible for both you and your wife to hold full-time jobs.

But what this does mean is that we should rack our brains for as many household outsources that we can afford—it will free up time in our schedules for both work and family. Look back at your log of how you actually spend your time and your analysis of it. What tasks were you willing to let someone else do without sacrificing any of your priorities? *Do you spend too much time grocery shopping?* Find a service that will do it for you; this may be as simple as working out a system with a local market that you call or fax orders to and it delivers them at a prearranged time. Or maybe you will want to regularly pick up preordered and ready-made dinners on the way home from work. (God knows, the cottage industry of gourmet ready-made dinners has mushroomed in recent years.) *Do you spend too much time doing laundry?* Again, find a service that will do it for you; it may seem like an "unnecessary luxury" at first glance, but it can go a long way to giving you free Wide-Awake Time to spend on those tasks and activities that you value more than loading the washer and dryer. We tend to be stingy with ourselves when it comes to such services; we associate them with rich, lazy people—but, heaven knows, we are neither rich nor lazy, just heavily pressed for the necessary time to be hands-on, productive workers *and* hands-on, productive fathers. Do not let yourself fall into the old calculus of figuring out if the cost of the service is covered, hour for hour and dollar for dollar, by your income. The only meaningful calculus is this: *does this service significantly help you achieve the life you want—that of a successful Marathon Dad?*

Some household tasks present some tricky questions. Take mowing the lawn. I, for one, get an inordinate amount of pleasure from doing this task: I like being outdoors, like the exercise (I don't use a rider), like the sheer mindlessness of it after a hard day's work. But six months of the year, this job takes close to four hours out of my week (I mow one acre a fifth of an acre at a time.) That's four hours I could be spending with my kids. Is the pleasure and recreation worth it? For the time being, I think it is. But next time I take my annual hard look at my schedule, I am going to have to ask myself again just how well mowing the lawn fits into my priorities.

Here's another tricky one: washing the dishes can conceivably be outsourced. (Actually, *any* household task is out-sourceable in principle; you may have to get creative to find the service or person to perform a particular task, but part-time workers are a glut on the market these days, so anything is possible.) Yet in my home, washing the dishes is a family activity that most of us (I cannot speak for *all* of my children) seem to enjoy. It's a regular time of chatting idly and joking while working together. Outsourcing this job *would* have an effect, however subtle, on our relationships, so I think it wise to keep this one in the family.

Once again, we are ready to fill in some blanks and to open up some found time in our proposed new schedule: tasks we feel we (or our spouses) should do and tasks we are ready to put out for bid.

Job-Sharing on the Home Front

And now we get to the really sticky part of all of this. *How do we go about fairly divvying up the tasks of home and child care with our wives?*

In the next chapter, we will discuss how to *negotiate* this distribution of jobs with our wives, but before we get to that point, we have to arrive at a position that we believe in—and that we believe in for good, well-thought-out reasons.

Let's start with a sobering statistic: Today, the average woman with a full-time job spends *twenty hours a week* on home-related tasks, while the average man with a full-time job spends *less than one hour* on home-related tasks. Granted, these devastating numbers are heavily weighed down by all those men who haven't the slightest interest in or intention of sharing the load equally—in a word, men who don't give a hoot about being Marathon Dads. Nonetheless, with a dispar-ity this great staring us in the face, we cannot ignore what is obviously a genuine trend any more than we can take comfort in the fact that we are bucking this trend—*not if we are still far from reaching parity with our wives on home-related tasks.*

In her seminal book on working mothers, *The Second Shift,* Arlie Hochschild describes with acerbic accuracy what she calls "The Egalitarian on Top, but Traditional Underneath Marriage." She is referring to those all-too-common marriages where the guy talks the talk of gender equality, but when it comes to sharing tasks, he manages to do anything but walk the walk. To pull off this little trick of denial, he cleverly recycles many of the myths we examined in Part I, like the myth of "Why Upset the Balance when She's Got It All Under Control?", the myth of "A Child Needs Her Mother More than Her Father," or the myth/alibi of "No One Ever Taught Me How to ＿＿＿ (Fill in the blank: 'change diapers,' 'buy kids clothes,' 'fold laundry' . . .)" What is more, as we have seen, the wife can help her equality-talking man shirk his share of the tasks by throwing up all kinds of obstacles to relinquishing the control she prizes. But, gentlemen, we are far beyond these little tricks and delusions now. In fact, we are ready to face a whole new set of tricks and delusions that keep us from walking the walk of genuine equality.

Preeminent among these mind-tricks is the one that goes, *"I earn much more money at my job than my wife does, so I should not have to do as much work at home as she does."* Among other things, this alibi conveniently ignores the fact that women are notoriously paid less than men for equal work. There is an even more insidious variation on this mind-trick that goes, *"I work harder on my job than she does, so I need/ deserve more leisure time."* The question, of course, is, *what makes you think you work any harder than she does? Is it because you know that you feel so damned tired after a day's work, but she still seems to be going strong after a day's work?* Sorry, but this piece of circular reasoning doesn't cut it— because the basic reason she is still going strong after a day's work is probably because you are not helping and the job has to be done, whether she's dog-tired or not. Suffice it to say that no man (or woman) can judge who works harder at his or her day job, so that simply cannot figure into your dividing up the home-tasks calculus.

But what may figure in this calculus is *who works more hours* on his or her professional job—including work done away from the office for his or her job. A man who works fifty hours a week at his job while his wife works twenty hours a week at her job can reasonably expect to spend fewer hours doing home and child tasks than she does. Yet before you run with this one, examine carefully exactly *why* you spend more time on your job than she does. *Is it because you are less willing than she is to ask for and take time away from your job so that you will have more time to share home duties?* If so, and if your wife would really prefer to spend more time at her job than she is now if you would take up more of the slack at home, then the answer to "Who works more hours?" probably suggests that you should be thinking about working *fewer hours on your job* and *more hours on the home front.* (More about the option of fewer hours on your job in the next section.)

Still, when it comes to working out equity for home and child-care tasks, hours logged cannot be the only factor in the balance. One fundamental reason why a calculation of hours alone cannot do the trick is because some jobs are more desirable (and some more onerous) than others. For example, playing catch for an hour with Joey Jr. is probably more desirable for you than tutoring Joey Jr. in solid geometry for an hour. Or, to use another example, driving Toby to play school is probably more desirable than changing Toby's diapers and giving him a sponge bath. Obviously, there will be some differences between you and your wife about which tasks are desirable and which are not, and these differences will provide both of you with the easiest part of the distribution of home tasks: *tasks that you desire and she does not* (like playing catch with Joey) *go to you, and vice versa.*

Ah, would that it were all this easy, but this is where Just-

Do-What-You-Want-to-Do Time ends. Because it turns out that for the most part, you and your wife will probably agree on which tasks are desired and which are not. Therefore, *desired and undesired tasks will have to be sorted out fairly.* But before we start working with that, let's consider some other questions that need to be considered here.

What if you are willing to outsource an undesirable task, but your wife is not? It would seem that she, de facto, gets that particular job . . . but not necessarily. Say that the task in question is driving Molly to her orthodontist, whose office is a half hour away; and say, further, that your wife is of the opinion that these visits are so traumatic for Molly that she believes Molly should have a parent with her for comfort and solace, especially on the way home. You, on the other hand, think that Molly is old enough to handle this on her own, or at least in the company of a sensitive surrogate who does taxiing for your kids on other occasions. But then add to this mix that your wife's work schedule does not allow her to take Molly to the orthodontist, but yours does. Starts to get kind of dicey, doesn't it? I have no pat formula for solving this kind of situation, but I can say this with certainty: *'tis far better for your marriage to discuss this question with an open mind and heart than to pull the old "You want it, then you do it!"— end of discussion.* Not only is it better for your marriage, but, as we will see later, every concession you make can become a bargaining chip for the future.

There is another consideration that needs to come into play here, one that was discussed at length in Part I, the Dad-Is-Not-a-Mom phenomenon. There are many child-rearing and child-care tasks that we as fathers are better suited to perform than are our wives for a great number of reasons. Among these reasons are that we may have greater aptitude for these tasks (included in that better aptitude may be a more suitable temperament and world view), that we may be a better role model for the child in question in this particular task role, and that the child may feel more comfortable with us in this particular situation. It may be a good idea to take another gander at that section of the book now; it can be a major key to distribution of tasks between you and your wife.

Now we come to a more complicated part of divvying up tasks between Dad and Mom—sorting those tasks that come up *irregularly,* like that deal-breaker of them all, staying home with a sick child. Later, we will get into some of the backup options that you will want to consider using in such situations, but here we need to think about those times when those options cannot be used (and believe me, there will be many such times). Also, we need to define who is in charge of finding (or not finding) these options when the need suddenly arises. ("Hello, Mr. Evans? This is the school nurse at Housatonic School—Owen has a fever of 100 degrees and we need to send him home. Now.")

Every couple will approach this problem differently, depending in large part on whether either of you has a more flexible work-time schedule than the other. But if you are like the majority of full-time working couples, *neither* of you can claim superior flexibility for this one. So what you have to do is bite the bullet and find a way of sharing these troublesome tasks fairly. One way to do this is simply to alternate: *"I took off a sick-child day last time, so now it's your turn."* But the problem with this formula is that it does not take into account the particular exigencies that either one of you may have on the day when such an emergency arises. Say you have an important meeting with a client who has flown in from Chicago, but your wife has a report to write—which, conceivably, she could work on at home. Clearly, it would not make good sense for you to take off from work to pick up Owen just because it was your turn. Yet the problem here is that a dangerous pattern can subtly become established: your work demands seem to take precedence over your wife's virtually *every time* an emergency arises. Not fair.

Here is the solution I most often recommend to couples: keep a log of who takes time off for these emergencies. *Every three months, tally up who's done what. If the numbers are not equal (or almost equal), then you must do something to even things out in the next three-month period, even if it still seems to you that your time demands feel more urgent than your wife's.*

Does this method sound artificial and arbitrary? Never mind, it works. On the one hand, it provides some day-by-day flexibility; and on the other, it prevents an outcome that both of you want to avoid at all costs—namely, a nagging sense that someone is being taken advantage of.

There are other, less urgent but nonetheless irregular situations that come up which also have to be sorted out between the two of you—things like taking Joey Jr. to a dentist appointment or attending Molly's parent-teacher conference. These situations can be anticipated, usually a week or more ahead of time. Three fundamental rules of job-sharing and schedule-making at home apply here:

1) Decide which of you is going to handle these tasks as early as you can, and as close to when you hear about them as possible.
2) Put it down in your schedule book immediately (even if you are not the one elected to do this task).
3) Plan your weekly schedules *together* every week at a regular time (say Sunday evenings).

Now we can go back to filling in the blanks in our new schedule, but for now only in pencil, pending final negotiations with the wife. In sum, the division of home labor between you and your wife should be guided by equality of hours spent, equality of desirable and undesirable tasks, plus a consideration of personal (and gender) aptitude and appropriateness.

A Few Words on How to Handle Unscheduled Events

What *do* you do when the school nurse calls you at work to say your son has a fever and needs to be picked up *and* it's your turn to handle such emergencies? Do you drop whatever you are doing and fly out the door?

Not necessarily. Once again, Super Mom has done considerable advance work on this issue. To begin with, she has a system of *backups* already in place for these contingencies, two or three layers of them, consisting of neighbors, friends, parents and in-laws, private baby-sitters, and baby-sitting agencies. What's more, she has *their* schedules handy at all times, as well as their phone numbers—she has these set for speed-dialing if her phone system has this feature. If her sick child needs to be picked up at school, taken home, and watched and/or nursed (or if this child simply wakes up too sick to go to school), she first determines if a surrogate would be appropriate (more about that important decision soon) and then, if she decides that is okay, she goes into action finding a backup to cover for her. Implicit in the deal with most of these backups is that Mom is on *their* list of backups for when they need subs for their own children.

Other backup preparations include making sure that your kids' school nurse has all the ways you can be reached: office phone, cell phone, beeper. As well, young children should always have a *laminated* card listing both parents' sets of numbers on their persons at all times. At home, preparation includes a constant supply of frozen dinners, a prominently displayed list of all relevant phone numbers, including those of your pediatrician, the ambulance service, and the other people on your backup list, and a list of protocols: "If Owen's temperature goes above 100, call me immediately. If Owen breaks out in hives . . . etc." Finally, if a backup is on duty for her, Mom calls in regularly—say every two hours—to make sure everything is under control.

This system can work very well for us too. Yet in my experience, many men face a psychological resistance to asking people to be part of their backup system and then to actually using these people when the occasion demands it. We males, as a general rule, have a real problem asking for help, especially voluntary help, and most especially voluntary help from our male friends. Calling up a friend and saying, "Hi, Hal, can you pick up Owen at school and bring him home for me?" feels to some of us like saying, "Hi, Hal, I am an utter and complete wimp who can't seem to get anything together. Help!" In short, the Wimp Factor again. (Obviously, most of the names on *your* backup list will be the same as those on *your wife's* list, but this does not seem to make this option any easier for many men.)

What can I say about this resistance except that I fully understand it, but it is time to put that behind us in the name of a civilized lifestyle. Just ask for this kind of help when you need it and give it back when you can—it is not really so hard once you get the hang of it.

Okay, now for the subtler problem of determining when a backup is acceptable to you and when no one but you should be there for your kid. The extreme cases are fairly easy to figure out:

The school nurse calls and says Owen says he has a headache, but no fever or other signs of illness; still, she thinks he should go home. At work, you have pressing business involving other people who are difficult to reschedule.

No problem. Call up a backup and check in frequently.
And at the other extreme:

The school nurse calls and says Owen (who is only six) has a fever of 101, is vomiting and crying. At work, you have pressing business involving other people who are difficult to reschedule.

No options. Apologize to your clients, find a backup associate to cover for you, and get to your son ASAP.
But, alas, not all such emergencies are so cut-and-dried.

What if the school nurse calls to say that Owen has a headache, but no discernible signs of illness, yet the boy is crying uncontrollably. Do you drop everything or not? This one is a highly individual judgment call. You'll probably want to consider Owen's general state these days. Is it unusual for him to cry? Is he going through a bad patch of insecurity? If so, do you think running to fetch him yourself is the best idea? Or do you think that action might set up a pattern of dependence that you believe would be best to squelch now? You may want to get your wife's input on this one.

But a word of caution here: in no place is the difference between a mom and a dad more evident than in the interpretation of what constitutes an emergency and what does not, with moms clearly tending to see more events as urgent than dads do. It is another instance of moms stressing caution and emotional support in child rearing vs. dads stressing taking risks and learning independence in child rearing. My advice is this: unless your wife is adding some new information for you to consider in your decision—that Owen has been having nightmares lately, which you didn't know about—I think it's best to stick to your own instincts and priorities here. The bottom line is that if you and your wife are sharing these "emergency" duties, you must be trusted to make your own decision on what constitutes an emergency.

Whatever decision you do make, my general advice is to arrive at it as quickly as possible and then put it into action without guilt or hesitation. Although the emergency may appear overwhelming at the particular moment it arises, chances are that in the grand scheme of your child's life and yours, whatever decision you make will not have long-range repercussions.

One question that often crops up when you opt for a backup is whether your child needs to be at home in his or her own bed, or whether the surrogate's home and guest bed will suffice. (Most people on your backup list will likely have children of their own; that's why *you* are on *their* backup list.) With very young children, this may be a difficult decision to make, but I believe that if you and your wife have decided to make this backup system a part of your lives, you should begin training your child early to feel at home at a friend's house, even when your child is feeling somewhat ill. It is not a hard adjustment for most children to make, especially if it becomes a part of their lives early on.

Getting back to the question of "to backup or not to backup," what if your child's emergency is at the low end of the scale, yet you do *not* have pressing business at work and the only item involving other people on your schedule is a tennis game? My guess here is that a quick review of your priorities would probably put your kid's need above your recreation, no matter how much you had been looking forward to this game.

Job-Sharing, Paternity Leave, and Other Hours That Can Be Subtracted from Your Work Schedule

We now come to the most dreaded topic about time, and I can already hear chairs screeching and feet scraping at the rear of the room.

"Look, I'm willing to pull my fair share of the load at home," one guy says, speaking for many, *"but I'll be damned if I'm going to risk my job and my career by asking for job-sharing or paternity leave or even one afternoon off a week. That would simply be unprofessional."*

Yes, in the old work culture and by the old rules, such options *would* be unprofessional. But as we have already seen, that culture and those rules are in the process of change *right now*. And I hope for all of us that this process will continue apace. One important way we can help keep that process going is by actually partaking of the work-schedule options that have opened up to us in the past few years. Another important way is by leading the path in our workplace to other creative changes that make it possible for us to be fully engaged, productive workers and fully engaged, productive fathers and husbands. (We'll delve more into these leadership opportunities in Part III.)

But let me get back to the fellow who says he is "willing to pull my fair share of the load at home" but doesn't see the need to "risk" his job in the process. My first question for him is fairly self-evident:

"Are you absolutely sure you can *pull your fair share at home without making some scheduling changes at work?"*

Perhaps you can—say by dropping other things from your schedule like recreational activities or by spending less time alone with your wife or, many men's first option, by doing with several hours less sleep. (Beware the Exhaustion Factor!)

But then again, if you have, say, two or more preschool-age children, your wife works at her job fifty hours a week not including commuting, and you either cannot afford or do not desire to leave your children's care largely entrusted to surrogates, there is a very good chance that you are going to have to look carefully for ways that you can spend fewer hours at your job. Remember that pause-giving statistic: in most families, the working mother spends twenty hours on home and child care, while the working dad spends an hour or less; to get those numbers near parity, the average guy is going to have to come up with *ten more hours a week!*

Before we weigh specific work-schedule options that may be available to you, let's return to some of the "Head" adjustments you will need to make in order to give these options fair consideration. Earlier, we looked into such mind-foggers as the Wimp Factor and other irrational fears on the job, along with unnecessary guilts at home. Now we need to consider some fundamental questions about how you see yourself as a professional worker.

For starters, ask yourself: *am I taking on more responsibilities at work than I need to in order to perform my job well?*

And the ancillary question: *am I spending more hours on the job than I need to in order to perform my job well?*

Both of these questions bring up the issue of Quantity of

Time vs. Quality Time *on the job.* As I have said, many of us were quick to adapt the idea of Quality Time to child rearing, but were blind to its more suitable application to the workplace. At work, too many of us have fallen into a "putting-in-time" mind-set, rather than the more effective *and* more efficient "accomplishing-the-necessary-task" mind-set.

The next questions have to do with the Career and Family Timetables that I introduced earlier.

Am I at a point in these timetables when my children need more of me and my wife needs more help from me than either will need in the foreseeable future?

Or, *Am I at a point in these timetables when it is especially critical for me to prove my worth at and dedication to my job if I am going to achieve the career goals I have set for myself?*

For most of us, the reflexive answer to this last question is that we are *always* at a critical point in our careers—it's a dog-eat-dog world out there and if we slack off in any way, we'll lose our place in line. My reply to this is twofold:

First, I believe that most of us grossly exaggerate how much we would really stand to lose in the grand scheme of our careers if we were to spend a year or two (or more) *not* devoting virtually all of our time and energy to them. No, chances are you will not lose your place in line if you negotiate for paternity leave for four months after your child is born— especially not if before and after that leave you do a first-rate job.

And second, take another gander at your priorities, gentlemen. If you value your family right up there with your career (and you probably do or you wouldn't be reading this book), you must consider every option you have in order to satisfy that priority. And if you are looking for inspiration, the business page of your newspaper seems to carry a new story every week of some high-ranking corporate executive who has decided that his family comes first and therefore he is stepping away (or partly away) from his job to spend more time at home. In recent years, Robert Reich wrote in his memoir that as Secretary of Labor, he did not have enough time for his young family, so he resigned; and the CEO of Pepsi-Cola, Christopher A. Sinclair, also dropped from the top spot to be the father he felt his children needed him to be, to mention only a couple of examples. These men recognized that a father's role required the same kind of time and energy that they had put into their careers.

The final question you need to ask yourself here gets right to the nitty-gritty of the whole enterprise of being a Marathon Dad:

Do I have enough confidence in myself as a first-class, productive, and responsible worker to believe that I can be highly valuable to my employer/co-workers even if I take advantage of the new scheduling and time-off options that are available to me?

And the ancillary question: *can I maintain that confidence in myself even if other people at work automatically assume that any man who takes advantage of these options cannot possibly be a consummate professional?*

In other words, do you determine your worth or do you let others do that for you? Hint: *don't let anyone else answer this question for you.*

Okay, let's consider a few of the most popular job schedule-change options:

Working at Home: With the advent of fax machines, e-mail, easily installed multiple-phone lines, portable phones, answering machines, computers, and a host of other electronic communication devices that are currently whizzing down the pipeline, this option is rapidly changing the MO of millions of workers of all kinds—not just working parents. It can often be a win-win for employers and workers alike: the employer saves money on space and utilities (although you will want to build some compensation for your home-office expenses into your deal with your employer); and you, the worker, can be on the home site to either actively participate in child care or oversee a sitter who is the hands-on caregiver. This latter option has proved extremely popular with fathers of preschool children: they are right there to do "dad" stuff, but if they need several hours of uninterrupted time, they've got it.

Clearly, this option does not work for every type of job, certainly not one that requires ongoing teamwork or the use of site-specific equipment or machinery. But for a surprising number of jobs, it is a perfect fit. Many fathers I have spoken to use this option for only part of their on-job time; they appear at the job site for meetings, conferences, and for face-time with clients. But the big payoff for these fathers is that they can work their schedules so they can be at home for those periods when it counts the most.

One unexpected bonus of this option for both employer *and* worker is that working-at-home time has clearly proved to be a highly efficient and highly effective use of time. Many men expected that the interruptions and distractions of home life would take a heavy toll; on the contrary, it appears that for most men, the interruptions and distractions of the *office* (people dropping into your office to chat, the old water cooler time-waster, etc.) are on the whole far more disruptive. Sure, you will miss some of the camaraderie around the cooler, but what you *won't* miss is Junior's first steps.

The working-at-home option can potentially be adapted in conjunction with most other options: for example, paternity leave (you work all or part of the time at home just for this period) and job-sharing (you divide job functions with a co-worker so that she or he does all on-site stuff while you do all non-on-site stuff). Most significantly, the working-at-home option is one you may want to elect for just *part of your career*, for those months or years when it seems most appropriate to your children's development timetable, to you wife's career timetable, and to your own.

Job Sharing: Super Mom was the pioneer for this option too, which is basically two people with the same duties working part-time who combine and coordinate their efforts so that together they produce the work results of one person working full-time. Again, data show that two job-sharing moms are very likely to produce higher quality and quantity work than a single person doing the same job full-time. The reasons for this are fairly self-evident: someone working four hours a day on the job is likely to be more focused and less fatigued than someone doing the same job eight hours a day.

Men, in general, have proved far less willing than women to take on *any* part-time job options, even for limited periods of time. Some of our reasons for this make good sense: first, fair or not, in general we are better paid than our wives, so it may make more economic sense in the family for the wife to opt for part-time work if you decide that one of you should do so for a particular period of your children's development timetable; and second, part-time workers often lose out on critical family benefits, like health insurance and pensions, so if your wife's full-time job does not adequately provide these, part-time work for you may not be an option.

But all that said, if your wife is earning as much or more than you are (the situation in an increasing number of two-worker homes), or if for whatever reasons the demands of your particular job or your career timetable are more flexible than your wife's *and* you both see the need for one of you spending more time on the home front for some period of time, then the job-sharing option should definitely be one that you consider. Obviously, finding a co-worker (especially a *male* co-worker) with whom to exercise this option may present problems—especially if the Wimp Factor holds sway at your place of work. But this is one of those situations that separates confident men from the sheep.

Flex Time: Anyone who has ever worked the night shift on a job knows the value of this option for the employer: it provides the most cost-effective use of work space. Recently, other types of work have expanded this idea of working during nontraditional work hours. For example, telephone salespersons are most needed between four and twelve in the afternoons and evenings; an employer who can find people who are willing to fill those time slots gets a bargain.

With the advent of working mothers and fathers, the concept of nontraditional work schedules has opened up a number of desirable opportunities for workers. Say, for example, that you and your wife have determined that you want one of you at home at three o'clock every weekday afternoon when the children come home from school. And posit further that you see a way in which both you and your employer can be winners if you go on a nontraditional time schedule, one that gets you home at three. This may mean coming in to the job each day at six or six-thirty; or perhaps it means putting in two or three hours of home-office work during the evenings after dinner. For men with employers who can spot a good nontraditional deal when they see one, this can be a fabulous option—especially during your children's early school years.

Minor Schedule Adjustments: If you genuinely find that you can manage to work full-time and be a dedicated, hands-on father who shares the home load equitably with your wife, there may be only minor work-schedule adjustments that you will want to make: say one or two afternoons each week you want to leave work at two-thirty or three so you can take your daughter to ballet lessons. This option is kind of a scaled-down variation on flex time. Today, an increasing number of employers are more than willing to accept such minor adjustments—especially if you systematically make up for this lost time by coming in earlier on those days, skip lunch hours, and/or put in additional work time at home.

More complicated are the minor adjustments you may want to make on a day-to-day or week-by-week basis. For example, you need to go to a parent-teacher conference at two o'clock this coming Thursday afternoon. Again, many of today's employers are more than willing to make exceptions for these circumstances, especially if they are not that frequent, and most especially if you give your employer and co-workers sufficient advance notice. *If you have made it your practice to note down these special family events* as soon as you hear about them, *and if you have made it your practice to keep* one *date book for both your home and job schedule, providing your workmates with sufficient notice will become routine for you.*

The unscheduled event of a sick child who needs parental care presents a special problem: namely, that you are unable to give anyone at work advance notice that you are going to take time off from work. Some companies are now building "sick-child leave" into their employment packages (although again, this is an option that far fewer men than women have taken advantage of for the usual "mind-set" reasons). Still, in this country most companies do not provide sick-child leave, or may provide an insufficient number of sick-child leave days for the average family of two or more preschool or school-age children. This is clearly an area where Marathon Dad needs to take a leadership role in forging change in the workplace; we'll explore how in Part III.

Paternity Leave: I have left this option for last in this section because I did not want to get booed off the platform before I had my say. As we have seen, we men appear to be terrified of taking paternity leave, even if our companies offer this option. I will not again trot out all the reasons that we tend to resist this one; by now you know what they are and you know what you have to do to get into the frame of mind for fairly considering this option. Here, I will lay out only the main reasons why this option may be the most significant one for you out there:

First, the initial four to six months of your child's life have been proved again and again to be critical to her development and critical to that miraculous business of bonding between you and her. You don't get to play catch-up with this one: you are either there most of the time for this crucial period or you are not.

Second, those initial months—especially with a first child—are so stressful, tiring, and generally overwhelming for parents that some time off for *both of you* can go a long way to help you maintain your sanity and your health, not to mention keeping your marriage from suffering. In Sweden, where the great majority of men partake of paternity leave (including immigrants from ultramacho cultures,) this option has been correlated with a decreasing divorce rate.

One last word about paternity leave: many surveys show that men with newborn children who do *not* use this option have a tendency to work significantly less effectively during the first few months of the children's lives—no doubt, one contributing reason for this is the sheer fatigue of being awakened three or four times a night. *Several months of poor performance on the job—now how's that going to affect your career?*

The Final Audit

Finally, we come to the grit of the nitty-gritty—*creating a schedule that works, taking into account everything we have now considered:* our priorities; our timetables and those of our family; an analysis of how we have been using our time (with special emphasis on wasted time); our hidden time needs and hidden time gains; the division of tasks with our wife; and our opportunities for spending less (or different) time at our jobs.

Even after we have given each of these considerations its due, when we actually sit down with a pen and a blank schedule sheet to fill in those blanks, we find ourselves confronted with difficult questions that need a definitive judgment and answer now. Such mundane, nuts-and-bolts questions as, *Who's going to take out the garbage? Exactly when? Who's going to take Owen to soccer practice? When? Are you going to wait at the field or come back to the house (or work) and do some other task?*

And harder questions like, *What am I willing to give up to find more time for what I want and need to do? The health club? Poker night? Job advancement this year?*

Only after you have filled in every fifteen-minute interval for a typical week in your life will you be ready to take your schedule out into the real world of Wife, Children, Employer, Co-Workers, and Subordinates. At that point, of course, be prepared to trash a goodly portion of your hard work in the harsh glare of Other People's Needs and Wishes.

14

Time Negotiations at Home

▼ ▼ ▼ ▼

Communication with Your Wife: "I'll Show You Mine if You Show Me Yours"

We've heard the phrase "Communication is the key to a good marriage" so many times that we barely listen to this cliche anymore. But it is time to listen up again, friends, because in a marriage of two working parents, communication is not only a key, it is a necessary condition for the marriage to function at all. And I am not referring to deep, psychological, revealing-our-innermost-secrets communication as much as I am referring to nuts-and-bolts, I'll-pick-up-Joey-while-you're-making-dinner-type communication. Without it, a working marriage, like any other functioning organization, will break down in missed cues, double duty, general inefficiency, and recriminations.

Incidentally, it also turns out that communication is the key to a good divorce—that is, a divorce that works well for everyone concerned, especially the children. All the negotiations discussed below should be worked through by divorced couples who want to share the tasks and pleasures of raising their children while continuing with their respective careers.

So our first rule is this: **set aside a big chunk of time ASAP to go over your proposed new schedule with your wife.**

This is the Meeting of All Meetings, the one where you hammer out the general distribution of tasks between the two of you. Below, we'll get into the ins and outs of that delicate negotiation. But before that, let's note our second rule: **set a regular time each week to review your schedules for that week.**

Sunday nights after dinner is the time most couples I know or work with choose for this rule. The outcome of this meeting should be a detailed schedule for the week for both of you in black and white, **each of you with a copy of the other's.** (I'll show you mine if you show me yours.)

Finally, a third practice I urge for every couple: **establish two or more regular "check-in" times during each day when you confer with one another about schedule events.**

I am referring here to quick communiqués of the "I'm leaving to pick up Joey now" variety. As much as anything, these quick hits serve as reassurances to the other partner.

The Meeting of All Meetings

When you sit down with your wife to discuss your proposed new schedule and proposed division of home tasks, it is best to start off by telling her exactly where you are coming from: *first,* that you want to work things out so that you can be a first-rate worker *and* a first-rate father and husband; *second,* that you want to work out the division of tasks so that *both* of you are satisfied and neither of you feels taken advantage of; and *third,* that you may have some different ideas from her about what tasks you are best suited to or are more appropriate for.

Let's consider this third point first. Obviously, what I am

basically referring to here are issues that were discussed at length in Part I, particularly in the section "A Dad Is Not a Mom." Many of these ideas will probably be new to your wife and, not to put too fine a point on it, at first blush some of these ideas may strike her as "piggy." They aren't, not if your overriding point is that you want to be fair and equitable, and that you believe dads have certain unique talents and functions in child rearing. In short, *you must be very clear that you have no intention of using these differences between dad-and-mom functions as an excuse for getting out of doing your fair share of work.*

Now let's go back to the second point, that you want to aim for a distribution of tasks that satisfies you both, that feels fair to both of you. This is a tricky area, as we have already seen: "hours-put-in" is not the only criteria for fairness; the relative desirability of tasks is important as well. What is helpful for both of you to acknowledge at the outset is that your aim is to arrive at *equal satisfaction* with your division of tasks, not necessarily some mathematical ideal of equality. To take an extreme example, if you both agree that your wife is only going to work part-time and do the lion's share of home tasks, then you are both okay—both satisfied. Or, to take another example, if you are at a point in your career where you feel that you can back off a bit without "losing your place in line," but your wife is in her first year on her first job, then you may both consider it fair that you are going to be more flexible with your work time than she is during the upcoming year—you agree that this is fair.

It is important to stress here that there are a whole array of tasks that fall under the rubric of "Being in Charge Of," as in "You're in charge of arranging for baby-sitters," or "You're in charge of organizing our vacation." Traditionally, all of these "in-charge-of" tasks have fallen to Mom, and there is still a tendency for both partners to leave them there. But there is no reason that they should not be distributed on the same basis as any other tasks.

Remember, there is not some third party at your meeting who is judging what constitutes an equal split; that determination is up to the two of you—and only the two of you. Abstract gender politics has no place at this meeting. I repeat, *fairness is what the two of you honestly agree is fair.*

Marital Monopoly

And now, let the games begin! Both of you should arrive at this Meeting of All Meetings with your own proposed schedule for a typical week. This schedule reflects what you each think is fair to the other and what you each think gives fair due to your kids and your respective jobs. If your schedules match perfectly, let the games end—you are literally one in a million. What is more likely is that your proposed schedules will indeed overlap in many areas, but not in others. Of these latter, many will probably turn out to be tasks you *never even considered*—tasks of the "Oh, you mean *you've* been changing the cat-litter box all these years?" variety.

But there will probably also be some tasks that you believed your wife enjoyed doing (or at least did not abhor doing) that turn out to be tasks she hates. This particular surprise usually comes about because you have fallen victim to a simple cognitive mistake. You think, *She must like doing that because—look—she's always doing it!* Now is the time for her to set you straight. It may also be the time for you to set her straight about similar assumptions she may have made about you.

And then, of course, there will be those tasks that you have selected because you firmly believe you are better suited to doing them—perhaps because you have more expertise or are more experienced at them. And there will be those tasks that you simply believe are better for a dad to perform with his child. As I've said, these proposed Dad-Should-Do-It tasks can pry open one hell of a can of worms. For example, say you have determined you need to spend more time with Joey Jr. now that he is entering adolescence, and that spending Dad

Time with him is crucial for his development. So you have set aside five hours a week to go horseback riding with him, an activity that you both enjoy and enjoy doing together—you are able to talk about things while riding along a trail that you somehow cannot talk about in other situations. Great, your wife says, but those five hours are going to have to come from somewhere—and there is a good chance they will come out of time during which you could be doing something else for the family or around the house. In other words, she's happy for you to do your dad thing, but not if it comes at the price of her having to do an extra five hours of tasks she doesn't really like doing. *That* does not feel like a fair trade-off to her, and rightly so. The only way to resolve this disparity is the same way to resolve all of these disparities: *by trading all of your tasks until you reach what genuinely feels like parity to both of you.*

Now is when you start playing Marital Monopoly in earnest. Working with fathers and couples over many years, I have found that the most effective way to do this is to *write down on* duplicate *sets of 3 × 5-inch cards all the tasks that need to be performed on the home front, along with all the activities apart from work that you simply want to have time for. Then each of you arrange your set of cards in four separate piles:*

1. *All* tasks *and* activities *you like doing and consequently want to do.*
2. *All tasks you think you should do, because of either expertise, experience, or Dad-Is-Not-a-Mom issues.*
3. *All tasks you really don't want to do.*
4. *All tasks you are willing to outsource.*

It's Monopoly time, as in "I'll give you Park Place for Ventnor and two railroads." In our game, it's "I'll trade you cat-litter duty for sorting-the-trash duty." And, "I'm willing to outsource grocery shopping if you place the food orders, and if you are willing to outsource laundry, I'll be in charge of getting it together and dropping it off at the Laundromat." And the more complicated, "You can take your five hours of horseback riding with Joey Jr., but I need more time for myself, say three hours each weekend when I can just stretch out and read without being disturbed."

The aim, of course, is to reach a point where you each feel the distribution of tasks from each category is fair. Along the way to this point, deals will undoubtedly be retracted and remade. Also along the way, some troubling stuff may arise, resentments that may have been smoldering beneath the surface for years. Be alert for them, and be prepared to deal with them in as positive a manner as possible—after all, now is the time when you can realign any imbalances in your relationship that are probably the reasons for these resentments.

One way to be alert to these hidden resentments is to keep your eyes open to visual, nonverbal clues that your wife isn't very happy with some of your assumptions. You may be able to tell only by a sigh or the look in her eyes or the shrug of her shoulders that she is deeply offended because you thought she actually loved changing diapers. Or you may be able to tell only by the way she taps her finger or looks down at the kitchen table that she thinks you are taking this Dad-Is-Not-a-Mom thing way too far for her, yet for one reason or another, she is loath to say so. Or, most dangerous, be vigilant for cues which show that although she is accepting a particular trade-off, in her heart of hearts she does not really feel that it is fair. My advice here is simple and important. *Do not let these cues pass by without doing everything possible to bring them out in the open—otherwise, they will come back to haunt you both later.*

On the other hand, try not to get sidetracked by these resentments. One or both of you may feel the need to "ventilate" a bit, as we psychologists delicately put it, but do your best to get back on track so you can use these feelings to inform your negotiations—*as hints to some level of unfairness felt by one of you that needs to be addressed now.*

It is also important for you to be alert to your own inner responses as the negotiations progress. Are you starting to feel overwhelmed by all you have to do to be really fair? Could this be a sign that you should be more open to outsourcing options? That you should be more flexible about taking time-off options that are available at work? Now is the time to be perfectly honest with yourself.

One final caution. Be as clear with each other as you can about what exactly each task entails. Too often, the day after these negotiations finds someone saying, "Oh, you mean getting Molly ready for school means packing her lunch too?"

The schedules you each end up with at the conclusion of the Meeting of All Meetings will become the templates for the weekly schedules that you work out each Sunday night. Most couples decide that both are happier if some tasks— usually those that neither particularly likes—are traded off every two months or so. And most couples also find that after the first six months, it is time for the Second Meeting of All Meetings—to consider some renegotiations now that you have each lived with your new schedules for long enough to know how these schedules really feel in lived time.

Communication with Your Children, or, How to Become a "Rap" Artist

There is a virtual library of psychology books written about how to talk with your children so that they understand you, and how to listen to your children so that you understand them. Many of these books are quite good (although a few I've seen patronize kids), but our aim here is to focus on only one significant area of communication between you and your children: *communication about time, particularly the time you spend together.*

But before I get into some of the subtler areas of Dad/Kid Time Talk, I need to lay out some Golden Rules that apply here—rules that are necessary preconditions for *trusting* communication between you and your children:

1) Inform your children as far ahead as possible exactly when you expect to spend time with them and when you will be unable to. For example, it should never come as a surprise to Molly *one day before* her dance recital that you have decided in the grand scheme of things that you need to be in Chicago to attend a business meeting. Of course, you may very reasonably make the decision that being in Chicago takes precedence over her dance recital—at least this time—but only in the very rarest circumstances will that be a decision that *you could not have made far ahead of time.*

2) Treat the time promised to/allocated to your children as sacrosanct as any other time you set aside for and promise to anyone else—including your work associates. In other words, treat time for them with *the same respect* you would for anyone else. Most of us know from past experience how easy it is to automatically treat Kid Time as the most flexible time on our schedules.

There is a third rule that comes into play only when your children are old enough to understand and use this information:

3) Let your children know what your total schedule is—where you will be and when. There is an obvious practical reason for this: a child with two busy, working parents needs to know where he can reach both of you when he needs to. Even if getting hold of you at unexpected moments is an option your child rarely uses—and in a well-organized family, they *will* be rare—every child requires the emotional security of knowing where his parents are at every moment of the day. This goes for teenage children too; they may deny it, but *especially* at this stage when they fly out the door to experiment with their new freedoms, they need the security of knowing where Dad and Mom are. It is especially important for you to let them know when you are going to be out of

town for more than a day and when you will be back; have them note this down in their own agenda books so that it never comes as a surprise to them.

But there is an ancillary part of Rule 3 that will make all of your communications about time with your children easier, happier, and on a more equal footing: Let your children know exactly how you spend your time away from them and why. I have found that the very best way to get this information across to your kids is to bring them to work from time to time so that they can see exactly what you do with your time there. Just once a year may be enough to get the basic idea across to them, but I believe every father (and mother) should initiate this practice with each child by the time he or she enters second grade. Not only does it take the mystique out of your daily absences and make you "realer" to your children in the process, it also almost always has the effect of relieving your children of unconscious or nascent feelings of abandonment they may experience when you do go out the door each day. Instead of thinking (albeit unconsciously), *Dad's leaving because he doesn't want to spend time with me,* your child realizes, *Dad's leaving because he has important things to do in his life, just as I have important things to do in mine.* Obviously, this is something you can *tell* your children—I can still hear my own father saying, "I've got to go now because I've got to make a g—d—living!" But in the case of explaining how you spend your time at work, *showing* communicates much, much more to your child than simply telling.

As your children grow older, you may want to start telling them how you *feel* about the time you spend doing what you do, the good feelings and the bad. For example, "I love going to those out-of-town sales conferences—I get to stay in a nice hotel, meet interesting people from all over, and learn lots of useful stuff for my job." Or, for another example, "I hate going to those out-of-town sales conferences—it's always the same old people with the same old stories and lots of lousy food, but it's crucial for my job, so I grin and bear it." Each of these messages is instructive in its way for your child. In the first, he learns that you like what you are doing, that you find a particular part of your job engaging and interesting. It is good for your child to learn that you go to work for reasons besides just earning money; to introduce your child to the idea of feeling fulfilled by your work. This kind of modeling can go a long way toward motiving your child to dream enthusiastically and constructively about his or her own future. But if you have delivered the second message, you also have conveyed something important—namely, that a person has to do some things simply because they are required of him and that this is part of what being responsible is all about. (Let me caution you here, though, that if *too many* of your communications are of this latter variety, you are basically conveying to your child only your discontent, and you could end up emotionally burdening your child with your unhappiness.) Again, underlying both of these messages are the very real *reasons you spend time away from home*, something that every child needs to understand.

The Critical Question Few Dads Ask Their Kids

Have you ever asked your son or daughter, *"If we could spend more time together, what would you like us to do?"*

Probably not—not if you are like most dads. Yet this is a fundamental question that has the potential to open our eyes to what our children really want from us, as compared to the inevitable preconceived ideas we have of what our kids want from us—often ideas based on our *own* childhoods.

One reason we tend to avoid asking this question is that we are afraid to hear the answer, afraid that our child will say, "Gee, Dad, I wish you would drive me to soccer practice every Tuesday and Thursday afternoon, and that we could play catch every night after dinner, and that every Friday you would take me and my gang out for pizzas and then go bowling, and that . . ." And we would just sit there feeling increasingly guilty because we have not come close to doing all of those things, nor could we imagine concocting a schedule that now includes them. Worse, we would feel that by simply asking the question, we have set our kid up for disappointment. In short, we believe we both would have been better off if the question had never been raised.

But I am sure you would still be better off asking this question. Especially if your child is mature enough to understand that the question *is* hypothetical—that, in fact, you can afford to spend only a certain amount of time with him. Because what you very likely will learn from his answer is what *his* priorities are. You will discover in what areas of his life he would most like to have you, giving you a far better idea of how to schedule your limited time with him.

All of this offers you a good opportunity to reciprocate and tell your child what, if the two of you could spend more time together, *you* would most like to do with him. Your response may open *his* eyes to companionable activities he never considered before, activities he never knew you liked or hankered to do with him. *"Gee, horseback riding? Wow! I didn't know you were into that, Dad."*

Either in this conversation with your child or simply in the scheduling decisions that come up for each of you in your day-to-day lives, conflicts inevitably arise. For example, you say to Joey Jr. that you want to spend some of your time with him helping him with his homework, in part because he is not doing as well in school as you think he should. Joey Jr., on the other hand, doesn't want you "in his face" while he's doing his homework—and anyhow, if you are going to spend only a certain amount of time with him, he'd much rather that time be spent at the driving range.

My first suggestion here is hear him out. If he thinks you are really listening to him, he may feel free enough to express to you exactly why he doesn't want you to monitor his homework, and his reasons may, in fact, be compelling. (*"I get so nervous trying to do my math with you that my brain goes on strike.")* Next, you might try to make your child a partner in figuring out how to resolve this conflict so that you both feel okay about it. You tell him that you want to make sure he does his homework and does it well, but that you really would like to spend more time on the driving range with him. *"How can we get there, Joey?"* You will probably be surprised at how creative your child can be when presented with a problem in which he has so much at stake. *"Tell you what— I'll do my homework by myself while you do something else. Then when I'm finished, you check it over, and if it's okay, we go to the range."* Sounds like a good solution to me.

Discussions such as the one above can afford you the opportunity to mentor your child in a skill that will take him a long way in life: *Time Management.* You can help him arrange his time so that he gets the most out of it—in this case, satisfying his responsibilities (homework) while satisfying his desires (driving golf balls). If he is old enough, you may even want to introduce him to that basic time management tool, a weekly, hour-by-hour schedule book.

Task Talk with Your Kids

An outsource resource that I have not mentioned so far lives in the bedroom across the hall from you—your kid(s). It may be hard to believe, but it was not that long ago when one of the prime reasons people had children was to help work the farm or run the shop, not to mention help chop the wood, prepare the meals, and feed the horses. I know it may sound outdated to some people, but I am a firm believer in keeping this tradition alive, albeit in a markedly reduced form. Not only does this practice help two overworked parents manage the load, it serves as a fundamental object lesson in personal responsibility for your children. I suggest that you initiate your kids in helping out as early as possible, say at about six years old, with simple tasks (making beds, putting dirty clothes in the hamper). Once the general idea that everyone has to pull his load is established, you can add tasks as the kids grow up, so that they graduate to dish washing, lawn mowing, laundry, and meal preparation.

But outsourcing tasks to kids brings up another area of time talk, one that seems to get dicier as the kids get older. Again, when you present your child with a task, hear out any objections he may have. Perhaps he'd rather switch jobs, say do the dishes instead of baby-sitting his little sister on Saturday nights. If his counteroffer is reasonable and it is manageable for the rest of the family, be flexible enough to go for it; but if his counteroffer is unreasonable and doesn't work with everyone else's schedule, be strong enough to tell him so. Any task you select for your child must be doable by him; if it is beyond his strength or abilities, there will be frustrations and disappointments all around. Also, be very sure that you have supplied him with the appropriate tools needed to do the task, like, for example, a lawn mower with sharpened blades and an adequate supply of gasoline.

Once you have decided on what job is his, make the task and your expectations about it *perfectly clear—what exactly needs to be done, how it should be done, and by when.* The purpose for this, especially with teenagers, is obvious: you've got to leave them as little "wiggle" room as possible; otherwise you will be rewashing every dish or watching the grass reach hayfield heights.

One final word about talking with our children about tasks: beware that perennial problem, Mom-Dad Splits. Say you remind Joey Jr. that he hasn't done the dishes this evening, and he says that Mom said he didn't have to because he has so much homework. First, go straight to the source. Did Mom really say that, or only something that sounded to Joey like that? And if, in fact, Mom did say that, refresh her memory about the schedule that you two have so painstakingly worked out, one that included "outsourcing" dish duty to Joey. There is a point where flexibility has to stop, and the kitchen sink seems to me like as good a place as any. My point is simply that you and your wife should always try to avoid overruling each other, and one way to ensure this is for both of you to stick to the basic task-division schedules you have agreed upon.

15

Loving Parents and Partners

▼ ▼ ▼ ▼

Now that we are all convinced that the ideal marriage is like a perfectly balanced business partnership, let us take a moment to remember the *real* reason we got married in the first place. It was not simply to create an efficient business relationship, was it? It had something to do with love—love and lust and joyful companionship.

Didn't it?

How quickly we forget, especially if we are in a perpetual panic over simply getting through each day with our jobs and families intact and functioning. Who even has the time to think about those quaint concepts? *"Love? Lust? Joyful companionship?* Give me a break. Not only have I got the McDougal report to finish, I need to pick up Joey and take him to the dentist." It is little wonder that marriages split asunder under the weight of a job *plus* fathering and mothering responsibilities—divorce can actually seem like a way to make our lives simpler and more manageable. (Of course, divorce rarely does have the effect of making life simpler, *especially* when there are children involved.)

And so, gentlemen, I urge you: try, always, to remember why you married her. And try, always, to keep those reasons alive and a significant part of your daily life. For Marathon Dad, this means being conscious of two distinct kinds of love for your wife: a) your love for her as the co-parent of your children; and b) your love for her as an individual, totally separate from your roles as parents.

The Folks Who Live on the Hill

For most of us, the idea of marriage always implied having children together, and in some ineffable way, we probably invoked this design in our decision to marry this particular woman: we actively chose her to be the mother of our children.

So it is that when we do have children and raise them together, we form a bond with that woman that is unlike the bond we have with any other adult. *By God, we created these little people together, you and I. We created them together, are nurturing them together, and are suffering and reveling in our parenthood together. . . . Now isn't that remarkable?* This bond creates a unique form of love—the devotion, dedication, and mutual appreciation of co-parents.

With all the stresses of work and parenthood, it is comforting to know that this particular form of love grows as we become more committed and adept at being Marathon Dads. On the one hand, the more involved we become with our children, the more we appreciate what our wives are doing for them, the nurturing care they give to them. And on the other hand, the more we participate in the tasks of bringing up the children, the more our wives appreciate, respect, and love us. Instead of feeling exhausted, overstressed, and resentful toward us for not doing our fair share, our wives feel better both about themselves and about us. It creates a cycle of co-parent love: you (Dad) did your share, so she (Mom) feels grateful and appreciative, and now she, in turn, acts more warmly, generous-spirited, and loving toward you, so you, in turn, want to do more to make her happy. What we have here is the exact reverse of the Cycle of Resentment that bedevils marriages in which the tasks of parenthood are less than equitably divided.

Another special loving bond you have with the mother of your children is this passionate common interest you share with no one else in the world with anywhere near the same intensity—to wit, the interest in your children. That means that your wife is the one person with whom you can indulge your desire to talk at incredible length about your children—to go over and over and *over* the fact that little Jimmy finally learned how to tie his shoes, or to discuss ad infinitum what you think of Greta's new boyfriend. Or, to put it another way, your wife is the one person in the world with whom you can have these conversations without boring her to death. Face it, when other people go into rapt detail about their kiddies' lives, you start to glaze over pretty quickly. Well, believe it or not, that's the way other people feel when *you* go into rapt detail about *your* kiddies' lives. That is, everybody except your wife.

This not only means some gratifying and indulgent gloating over your children's accomplishments—which happily often involves mutual stroking for fathering and mothering well done—but it also means some down and dirty complaining about the kids. Again, if anybody other than your wife were this critical of your children, if they were to say, for example, that Joey is turning into a spoiled brat, you would be absolutely furious. But, hey, when it's us-against-them time, part of the parental bond is being allies in complaining about the children and in asserting your rights vis-à-vis the little monsters. Sometimes it is strangely heartwarming to know that your wife thinks Joey is turning into a spoiled brat too.

This brings up another special bond between parents—you look to each other for reality checks about the children, a sort of cognitive confirmation. For example, when Joey leaves the dining room with a certain expression on his face that for all the world looks to you like a spoiled brat's smirk, you turn to your wife for confirmation. *Did you see what I saw, or am I reading too much into it?*

In a word, being parents together is an intense form of intimacy. And intimacy, even if it is cobbled out of conversations about Jimmy's shoe-tying and Greta's boyfriends and Joey's smirks, is the basic stuff of love.

Hey, Remember Me?

But while you are remembering why you married your wife in the first place, it is a good idea to also recall those qualities that attracted you *other than* her potential as the mother of your kids. Like her smile and the turn of her ankle, her laugh, her encyclopedic knowledge of the films of Doris Day, her love of Mexican food. All those things that made you fall for her, but that too quickly became obscured by the day-to-day travail of your jobs and child rearing.

To this end, you need to consciously set aside time together away from the children, time when you don't even *talk* about the children. Although being joined at the hip as parents is an intimate bond, it can also be a bind that keeps you from seeing your wife as the Romantic Other, or as the Object of Your Lust, or as your Loving Pal who has a life away from the children that needs to be shared and supported. Somehow we find it easier to nail down time for our children than for each other. Let's try to change that. Schedule your No-Kid Time together with the same care and resolve that you schedule the other events in your busy lives. This time together may be romantic dinners out, movie dates, or weekends without the kids at an inn or hotel. But it may also be a non-kid project such as working together on a political campaign, making Christmas cards, or painting the guest room. Whatever it is, make an effort to avoid the temptation to yak just a little bit more about the children. If you talk at all about them— say on that romantic weekend at a country inn—make it something like, "The kids are in great shape. We did good. So now let's forget about them for forty-eight hours and just enjoy each other."

One final tip: try to have one phone conversation with your wife each day that eschews all kid-talk, a conversation in which neither of you eventually says, "So, are you picking up Joey or should I?" Amazing how refreshing that can be for your relationship.

PART III

POLITICS

▼ ▼ ▼ ▼ ▼ ▼

Taking the Lead to a
Marathon-Dad-Friendly Work Culture

16

Talking the Talk and Walking the Walk

▼ ▼ ▼ ▼

To be sure, the negotiations we have at home with our wives and children are political in one sense, but I have reserved the Politics section of this book for the most political part of Marathon Dad's life: *the workplace.* It is in the workplace where we will meet the greatest resistance to the changes we need to make to be successful Marathon Dads; it is in the workplace where we will have to do our most creative work to translate our priorities into effective practices; and it is in the workplace where we will have to assume the mantle of leadership if we are going to be an agent of change in the transformation of the mind-sets and policies of the old work culture into a new, progressive, father-friendly culture. In other words, if we genuinely want to put everything we have learned into practice, then our offices and factories and building sites are where, above all, we will have to start talking the talk and walking the walk of Marathon Dad.

Nietzsche said that the true Historical Hero is the man who anticipates the coming *Zeitgeist* (the spirit of the times) and then leads other men to embrace that change and use it effectively. We Marathon Dads stand at the threshold of a new period in Family and Work History. We see it coming, and so we are in the position to be among the first to enter this new period and set the course for those who follow. If this statement sounds a bit grandiose, I do not mind in the least, because I believe it to be true. The coming changes in the way men of intelligence, imagination, and heart look at their lives both at work and at home, *and* the coming changes in the culture and structure of the workplace, are major historical changes. The men who recognize these changes and who have the guts to seize the new day will, indeed, be true Historical Heroes.

The Deal It Is A-changin'

"Downsizing"—that '90s word strikes terror in the hearts of men from the conveyer belt all the way to the highest reaches of management. For a while, the wordsmiths in the corporate policy departments tried to take the sting out of this bottom-line strategy by renaming it "right-sizing," but for those of us whose jobs were suddenly on the line, both words meant the same thing: job security was out the window.

Job security was the prime condition of the employer/ employee contract of the corporate culture in which many of us came of age. The deal was elegant in its simplicity: if we provided our employers with hard work, long hours, total loyalty, and commitment, then we would be rewarded with job security, a decent paycheck, status on the job, and the prospect of advancement. But downsizing—the very real possibility that we could lose our jobs in spite of how hard or how long we had worked or how loyal and committed to the company we had been—signaled that the deal it was a-changin', and it was a-changin' big-time.

Yet for Marathon Dad, this is not necessarily bad news at all. Because implicit in that old employer/employee deal was that we could not even entertain the idea of having divided loyalties—a loyalty to our families that "rivaled" our loyalty to our jobs. In this old order, the number of hours we put in on the job was the very measure of our loyalty to it. Or, to put this the other way around, if we asked for time off from the job in any form whatsoever in order to take care of business at home, it was considered a sign of disloyalty by our employers, who felt not a particle of shame in deeming it so and penalizing us accordingly. In short, there was no way that this old deal could even begin to accommodate father-friendly policies.

At the same time that downsizing reared its ugly head, corporate policymakers were becoming conscious of the fact that the most significant bottom-line evaluation of their employees could be rendered not so much by looking at their time cards as by looking at the *results* of their labors—*the quality of the product, not simply the number of hours logged in.* The door was opening—at least a crack—to the idea of a more flexible approach to our work schedules, one that put the *quality* of our work performance ahead of *when* or *where* that performance took place. In this (very gradual, ongoing) change, father-friendly policies had found something of potential value to the employer.

Today, companies are in the process of changing the basics of the employer/employee contract. No, job security is not the same part of the deal that it once was, and it probably will not be again in the foreseeable future. But a new contract is developing that trades the quality of our performance (however we arrange to produce that quality) for those options that make our *total lives* more satisfying. Quality of life is what these employers are offering, and for the Marathon Dad who knows what he wants, this is the very deal he has been looking for.

Corporations which are in the vanguard—the ones being led by men who have the vision to see the *Zeitgeist* coming down the pike—are realizing that if they are not going to guarantee job security, they have to provide lifestyle satisfactions to their workers, and not just for the rank and file, but for top management too. Otherwise, these employees are going to look elsewhere for an employer who *will* provide these satisfactions. What's more, these corporations are also realizing that they stand to gain a host of bottom-line compensations by providing us with the policies that make our *total lives* more fulfilling. For starters, the old axiom that happy workers are productive workers applies here in spades. A working father who finds himself free of the stresses, tensions, guilts, and fears associated with trying to please Two Masters is a working father who can focus clearly on his work, take pride in the quality of his work, and feel unconflictedly good about making his employer happy.

There is another, subtler value to the employer that is only now emerging. As we will see, it takes some real imagination and problem-solving ability for Marathon Dad to create the best practices for satisfying all of his priorities. This creative approach to his whole life inevitably becomes an integral part of his headset, and he gets to be more creative on the job. Some of the energy that drives this creativity derives from the fact that the Marathon Dad who finds ways to make his whole life function in an optimum manner feels in control of his life and hence is much more confident and personally secure. So the bottom line now is that not only is he a more productive worker, he is a more creative worker too.

Creativity on the job becomes more and more valuable to employers because of another major shift in the workplace: the change from a *vertical hierarchical structure* (like a military chain of command) to a more *horizontal structure* (group work with shared judgments and decisions). The advent of horizontal structure is often considered part of the "feminization" of the workplace. Traditionally, women have found a cooperative, high intra-communication environment best for getting work done; with the influx of women to the workplace, this MO has taken hold and in the process been given high marks by many highly advanced companies. The main reason this structure is valued is because teamwork often engenders higher-quality, original thinking than individually produced, one-boss-evaluated work does.

Again, this is a workplace shift that has a high positive impact on Marathon-Dad-Friendly issues. Working in a team provides far better substitution and backup resources for us than the old vertical structure did. Expertise is shared: teammates know what our responsibilities and deadlines are; they know exactly how to fill in for us when non-job time demands take us away from work. In addition, in an increasing number of jobs, many of our teammates are likely to be women—in fact, working mothers. And these co-workers not only are naturally sympathetic to our home/child-care demands, they have expertise in innovative ways to balance home and work responsibilities that comes from working out this balancing act a good decade longer than most of us have. So it behooves us to listen up.

Making the Personal Political

Yes, the deal at work is changing, but the cold fact is that although these changes have set the stage for new Marathon-Dad-Friendly Policies, most companies are dragging their feet about putting many of these policies in place.

But that is not our biggest problem.

Our biggest problem is that even when these policies *are* in place, most men are loath to take advantage of them. We may talk the talk, but until we stop believing in our heart of hearts that "Paternity Leave Is for Girls," and until we realize that *real* men are not in the least intimidated by the Wimp Factor, we will never give these policies the consideration they deserve. And until we do that, all the talking in the world will not make a dent in the Old Workplace Culture.

It is an anthropological verity that culture always lags—and lingers—behind changes in policy. Policies are not people and only people can change the way a culture looks at and thinks about itself; only people can take the actions that transform the values of a culture. And that is precisely how Marathon Dad can become a Historical Hero—*by taking the actions and*

*setting the examples that change the culture of the workplace
into a place where a man can be a first-rate worker* and *a
first-rate father.*

But let's start with talking the talk, because that is the first
step we need to take to break the barrier of silence that often
surrounds Marathon Dad issues in the workplace. When we
publicly, unashamedly, and confidently start talking the talk of
Marathon Dad, we not only begin to get our co-workers and
bosses to look at issues from a new perspective, we also goad
ourselves to take the next step—walking the walk of Marathon Dad.

Talking points:

**1) Talk openly with your colleagues about your chil-
dren and your concerns about them.**

When we talk about our children at work, the topic is usually their achievements: "Hey, Joey made varsity football," or
"Molly got into Yale." Fine, but what I am referring to here is
more everyday stuff, and hence more meaningful stuff: "Joey's
having a hell of a time with fractions and I'm trying to figure
out what to do—get a tutor? Talk with his teacher? What do
you think?" and "I can't stand this gang of kids that Molly
hangs out with. They're a bunch of deadbeats and I can see
Molly picking up some of their habits. But what can I do? If
I say anything, she defends them."

Our first aim here is to get our colleagues' input. But beyond that, we are showing our concern for our kids and in so
doing, setting an example for others that it's okay to have
these concerns and to talk about them. And, most important,
we will be demonstrating that we can talk this talk without in
any way diminishing our work performance or our commitment to our job. In such casual conversations as these do our
priorities come out of the closet and does the culture of the
workplace begin to change.

2) Speak openly about your goal of doing your fair share on the home front, but at the same time NEVER use home obligations for producing less than first-rate results/product on the job.

I am not suggesting here that you make some pompous public declaration about what a raw deal working mothers have been getting and what a splendid fellow you are to pitch in—that would surely turn everyone off completely. But I *am* suggesting that when it fits into a conversation, you are able to say, for example, "My wife has been so stressed out lately with all she has to do at work and at home that I've decided to pitch in a whole lot more." In other words, in casual conversation you stand tall on your priorities and commitment to being a Marathon Dad *in spite of* any Wimp Factor responses your words will inevitably elicit. Here is where you confront the Wimp Factor head-on and stare it confidently in the face. Your attitude says, "I'm not afraid to do what I believe in, and as you can see, I'm no less a man for it."

Key to making this communication effective is the caveat that you never your duties at home as an excuse for doing inadequate or incomplete work on the job. You cannot be an agent of change if you are a shirker; heroes do not make excuses for anything they do consciously. Of course, this does *not* mean that if, say, you elect to take two months paternity leave, you will somehow be able to do the same quality work during that two-month period as you normally do—the fact is, you probably won't do *any* work during that period. But no excuse is needed. You are simply exercising a legitimate option to do something that you believe in; and before and after you exercise that option, you will put in a first-rate performance on the job. I repeat: no excuse or apology is needed here. Once again, a communication like the one above can set the wheels of work culture creaking forward.

3) Share the problems you have in trying to balance work and family responsibilities with your colleagues;

engage them in conversations about their own problems doing the same.

Here, I'm talking about concrete problems, like, "My wife can't get to Joey's parent-teacher conference Thursday afternoon, so I need to go. But I'm supposed to meet with a client that afternoon. What the hell can I do?"

Again, not only are you soliciting your colleagues' advice, but you are opening the door to the possibility of *openly discussing a problem that many of you undoubtedly share*. This one is a giant step in changing the culture of your workplace.

A number of consequences follow from such a communication. First, some colleague may come up with a practical solution that has the potential to establish new ways of cooperating on the job. For example, this man or woman might say, "I'm up to speed on that client's account and they know me, so I'll cover for you. You can do the same for me sometime"—*and you will*. Second, such communications serve as ground from which concrete political actions can follow; before you can organize like-minded colleagues to create and lobby for father-friendly company policies, you need to identify who these like-minded men are and begin the conversation with them about your mutual needs.

Walking the Walk: First Steps

The initial actions Marathon Dad takes are to invoke those father-friendly options that are already in place and to do so *without shame or apology*. But first, a critical distinction. There probably is no such category as "father-friendly policies" at your company because such options will be under the gender-neutral rubric of *"family*-friendly policies." Sounds wonderfully egalitarian and democratic, doesn't it? But beware of secret codes: most of these policies were initiated by Working Moms, and to this day most people—employers and employees alike—view them as specifically *mother*-friendly policies, *for moms only*. And the moms who exercise these options are generally viewed as "Mommy-Track Moms," women who will be satisfied enough by these options to keep working and working well, but who do not aspire to advancement to the top jobs. *That is not the deal that most of us are looking for—not by a long shot.*

Okay, let's say that your company has a "family-friendly" policy of offering unscheduled time off for child-care duty, emergency or otherwise. And you've got this parent-teacher conference you need to attend on Thursday at three o'clock, just the kind of situation that this policy was created for. There is only one problem: your boss (although he would probably never admit it) believes in his heart of hearts that this family-friendly option is really only for moms. You have surmised this from the fact that no other man has ever exercised this option (which may say as much about the guts of your co-workers as about your boss) and from the Wimp-Factoresque offhand comments and smirks that your boss regularly displays. How do you approach this guy?

1) First, approach him as far ahead of time as possible.

If you suddenly have a sick child you need to attend to, that doesn't give either you or your boss any lead time; but if it's like the above parent-teacher-conference scenario, there is no reason that you cannot tell your boss (and colleagues) about your time need weeks ahead. One reason that you may not tell your boss far ahead of time is that you keep putting off this conversation because you really are not looking forward to it. Never mind, just do it.

2) Go into his office with a plan for how your work will get done in spite of your absence.

Tell him, for example, that Frank is going to cover the client meeting, and further, that you plan to meet and/or talk with Frank that very evening in order for you to follow through with the client.

3) Be prepared to demonstrate to your boss how he and the company will benefit from your exercising this option.

The basic way you do this is by stressing the assurances in #2 above, plus explicitly expressing how much you appreciate the policy and what it will do for your life. Implicit in this expression of appreciation is the loyalty you feel toward the company and your job, and your willingness to go the extra mile when the situation demands it.

4) Finally, prove to your boss that you can exercise this option and still meet the demands of your job and produce high-quality work.

This one is after the fact—after you have left early that Thursday afternoon to attend the parent-teacher conference. Make damned sure that your substitute (Frank) has been well prepared to fill in for you and that you meet with him ASAP to discuss his meeting with your client so that you can follow up appropriately. The point is that you have to *prove* to your boss that everything you promised him would happen actually does happen; this includes showing your appreciation after you've exercised the option and coming through on any quid pro quos that you have promised or implied when you originally broached the request. In this way, more than any other that we have discussed so far, will you change the mind-sets and prejudices that have been limiting your superior's application of these policies to working fathers. Another giant step in changing the culture of your workplace.

Politically speaking, it is profoundly important that you let as many people in your workplace as possible know that you have exercised this option. *That is a necessary part of setting an example for others to follow.* Some of us may instinctively feel that it is better to keep this "special favor" the boss has granted us on the "q.t.," and, in fact, some bosses may even urge us to keep it under our hat. (This boss figures that if the

word gets out, *every* man will want to use the policy. *Exactly!*)
Again, if you are going to be an agent of change in the culture
of your workplace, you have to make your actions public statements. There is another, more practical reason why you will
always want to let everyone know when you exercise a family-
friendly option: in case there are unfair and/or illegal repercussions for your action, you need to have witnesses. (More about
that below.)

Clearly, requesting one Thursday afternoon off is a far cry
from exercising options for working at home, job-sharing, flex
time, or paternity leave. But the same guidelines apply for
each of these: advise your employer as early as possible when
you intend to exercise the option; explain in detail how your
job responsibilities will be met in the new arrangement; and
show how your company will benefit from having you use this
option. Remember, if the policy is there, you are entitled to
use it.

It almost goes without saying that when it comes to dealing
with your subordinates, you will take the same position on
Marathon-Dad-Friendly issues as you are urging your superiors to take. But as a leader of cultural change, you need to
go the extra mile and *suggest* to your employees when and
why they should exercise their options. Say that your subordi-
nate, Jim, just had his second child and you know that his
wife is entitled to only a one-month maternity leave at her
place of employment. You also know that this newborn is a
bit on the troublesome side—you can tell by the way Jim has
been dragging himself around the office since the birth. So
you call him into your office and talk to him about his option
of taking paternity leave for a month or two, starting either
now or when his wife's leave expires. You tell him to think
about ways in which his work responsibilities could be covered
during this period (perhaps the kind of work he does can be
done on a part-time basis from his home). You tell him that
you would expect him to return to work after the leave and
to pick up his duties with a first-rate performance. And you

tell him that everyone stands to benefit from this, including yourself and your colleagues. Finally, and most importantly, you tell Jim that if he exercises this option, you will stand behind his decision with your superiors and will do everything in your power to guarantee that he will in no way be penalized for exercising the option. In this way, you will not only give the culture of your workplace a major push forward, you will win the loyalty—and the fine performance that naturally follows from loyalty—from your workers.

Dealing with Dinosaurs

Okay, what about the dinosaurs? What kind of game plan do we need to prepare for the Boss-from-Hell, the guy who doesn't have a clue to what we are talking about when we utter words like "flex time" and "job-sharing," and when he finally *does* get a clue, cannot for the life of him understand why we would want to go through with such a noodle-headed plan and certainly cannot understand why in hell *he* should go along with it.

Well, **first,** this guy is not going to be swayed by any abstract policy razzmatazz. You need to put concrete, black-and-white information right in his face just to get his attention. This is a man (invariably a *man*) who values face-time over everything—either you are there where he can see you, doing your job, or you might as well not exist at all. You will have to demonstrate to this dinosaur that he is not going to be shortchanged by any new way of doing things, that if, say, you take flex time, you are not pulling a fast one on him and the company.

Second, teach this guy slowly how the new way of doing things works. Don't ask for the whole ball of wax right off the bat; rather, ask first for something fairly inconsequential—to leave at three-thirty on alternate Friday afternoons, for example, so that you can pick up your son at soccer practice. And then do everything in your power to prove to him that he does *not* get shortchanged or cheated by this arrangement. Do extra work to make up for the time lost; make sure that all your on-site responsibilities are covered by a co-worker. In short, cover your back real well.

Third, once the dinosaur is convinced that at least in this situation he's not being bamboozled, add another piece, e.g., that you are going to take alternate Fridays off entirely and do all your work from home. Approach it this way: "Let's try this Fridays-off thing for a month and then do a concrete evaluation in terms of productivity, profits, whatever, at the end of that period to see how it is working out for both of us."

In other words, the only way to do business with this guy is to *always come to the table with bargaining chips:* "If you give me this, I'll give you that. And afterward, we'll go over everything to make sure you've gotten your money's worth out of me."

You have to maintain a delicate balance with these prehistoric types. On the one hand, even if his obstinacy gets to you, you have to refrain from getting into a pissing contest with him. Remember, these guys are well practiced in intramural warfare; in fact, that is usually their only "A" subject. It just would not pay to get in a fight with him (at least not yet). But on the other hand, if you walk into his office like a pussycat, all "I'm-sorry-to-bother-you-but," he won't respect you enough to even listen to your proposal, because this guy is definitely predisposed to think that anything remotely Marathon-Dad-like is pure Wimpishness. So even if you don't stride into his office with a chip on your shoulder, you need to walk in there with a manly gait and determination in your eyes.

One other hint: you probably would do well to use the Broken Record Technique with these guys. I'm not implying that this kind of boss is *always* on the dim side; I've just noticed that dinosaurs often need repetition to comprehend an alien-sounding concept.

Boss-From-Hell: "Friday afternoon is usually a high-volume time for us, sorry."

You: "Let's just try it for a few weeks and see how it works out. I think I'll be able to cover everything."

B-F-H: "No one has ever done anything like this before—not even a woman—so I don't see any advantage in starting now."

You: "Let's just try it for a few weeks and see how it works out. I'm sure I'll be able to cover everything."

B-F-H: "Let me think about this for another month or two. I'll get back to you."

You: "Let's just try it for a few weeks and see how it works out. I know I'll be able to cover everything."

B-F-H: "Quite frankly, I don't see any value in this for the company. And I don't think you do either."

You: "Let's just try it for a few weeks and see how it works out. I'm positive I'll be able to cover everything."

Getting Tough

What if this B-F-H is flagrantly and deliberately going counter to existing company policy or even counter to the law? What if this guy is so out of touch and cocksure that he looks you in the eye and says, "Don't quote me on this because I'll only deny it, but if you take paternity leave, you'll be shooting yourself in the foot . . . I'll make sure of that"?

The time has clearly come to cease making reasonable proposals to this guy, to disengage that broken record. It is time to get tough.

First, immediately document what he said by repeating it to others and by writing it down. (Be sure to bring a colleague/witness with you at all future meetings with this guy.) **Second,** notify your union. **Third,** notify a lawyer, either your union's or your own personal lawyer—*because the threat this guy made to you is definitely actionable.* The lawyer may very well advise you to counter with a legal threat to this guy.

There is a time to get mad and show it, a time to fight like hell and fight to win, and this, gentlemen, is it. But when you fight to win, fight smart and fight within the rules. Show everyone that you are fighting to make the system work—to make it work better for *everyone* concerned—not to overthrow the system.

The Subversion Watchdog

There are sneaks among us—employers who have put father/family-friendly policies in their employee handbooks, but who find ways of discouraging workers, especially male workers, from using them. One of these ways is by giving poor or lukewarm Performance Evaluations to workers who exercise these father-friendly options. In a word, this is dirty pool, but probably few of you will be surprised that such devious practices exist.

But there is something we can—and *must*—do about these subversive activities. It will not be easy (hey, I never promised you a rose garden), but the Marathon Dad who is dedicated to fighting the good fight for all working fathers will add Subversion Watchdog to his responsibilities.

If you suspect that your Performance Evaluation or that of one of your co-workers or subordinates has been tainted in any way by the fact that a father-friendly option has been used, go into action:

1) **Gather all relevant information.** Ask around and dig into files for answers to questions like: *"Is there a history of poor evaluations given to mothers in this company who exercised these options?"*

   "Is there a history of poor evaluations given to other fathers in the company who exercised these options?"

   "Have mothers who exercised these options been put on the 'Mommy Track' (limited job advancement)?"

   "Have fathers who exercised these options been put on the 'Daddy Track'?"

2) **Make an honest evaluation of your own perfor-mance prior to and following your exercise of the option.**

Ask yourself, *"Did I give my employers adequate ad-vance warning that I was going to use this option?"*

"Did I satisfy every condition laid out in the company rules for exercising this option?"

"Did I arrange for my responsibilities to my job to be met either by me or by others during the period I exer-cised the option?"

"Did I give less than a first-rate performance prior to and following the exercise of this option?"

Ultimately, what you are asking yourself is, *Did I re-ceive a poor evaluation (or did I lose my place in line for job advancement) because of incompetency, lack of experience or expertise, or did I receive a poor evaluation for other suspect reasons?*

If the evidence for subversion is strong in your answers to both #1 and #2, it is clearly time to confront the powers that be. Some of you will want to do this via your union reps, others by approaching your immediate superior. In either case, present your position cogently, clearly, and coolly. Give them plenty of opportunity to mend their ways, but do not tread meekly; the law (*and* the coming *Zeitgeist*) is on your side. The Historical Hero knows that confrontation is inevitable when he is effecting real change.

The Political Gets Serious

There is nothing like an unjust Performance Evaluation to goad us to move beyond personal confrontation and to enter the realm of genuine political action. (Obviously, there are a great number of events that can trigger this stage, including the realization that your company does not have *any or a sufficient number of* father/family-friendly policies to accommodate the committed Marathon Dad in the first place.) It is time to gather the troops.

1) The first step you need to take is to identify all your work colleagues—*men and women alike*—who are also trying to find fulfilling lives that balance work and home responsibilities. If you've been talking the talk at work openly enough and long enough, most of these people will already be known to you. *Are there any men around who have successfully managed to be both first-rate workers and first-rate fathers?* Get the word out that you are looking for other Marathon Dads to join you in your quest.

2) Find out exactly what Marathon-Dad-Friendly policies and opportunities are already in place at your company. *Do they offer paid paternity leave? Flexible work schedules? Telecommuting? Part-time work options? Time off for sick-child care? For sick-elder care? Do they have on-site child care? A homework program for your children?*

Once you identify these, look for which ones are actually used and which are not—and why not. *Have some men fallen off the promotion track because of—directly or indirectly—their devotion to their families?* All of this will probably involve some real digging—reading endless, jargon-filled manuals and policy statements (if you need help here, ask a lawyer who does *not* work for the company) and questioning the company's Work/Family officer.

If your company does not have a Work/Family officer, why not? And if it does, does this officer have a real commitment to working fathers, or to working mothers only? What can you divine about his agenda—is he just there for public-relations purposes, or is he really mandated to help working fathers make their lives more manageable? Does this officer also have other responsibilities in the company? (I know of one company where the Work/Family officer is also in charge of Performance Evaluation! How's that for conflict of function?)

228 ▼ MARATHON DAD

Does your company offer Employee Assistance Programs for fathering problems? For stress management? Does it offer training seminars around fathering issues like homework, sexual development, drug abuse, dealing with teachers and school administrators?

Does your company work with the community and community organizations to support fathers—say by joining in establishing child-care facilities or underwriting homework hot lines?

And finally, are the managers at your company being trained how to be responsive to working fathers' needs? If so, is this training effective or just window dressing?

Take notes:

3) Singly or in a group of like-minded colleagues, draw up a description of the culture of your workplace as it exists now. Is there a premium on face-time in your organization? Do they value time-put-in more than performance and product results? Is total commitment to the job still the watchword there? Do they still reward committed workers with total job security? Do they value creativity? Is the place awash in creeping Wimp Factor-ism?

4) Meet with those colleagues who share your concerns. For starters, make these "unofficial" meetings that are off the premises and off company time. Also for starters, meet only with *male* like-minded colleagues. Later on, for sure, you will want to consult and join with the working mothers in your company who share your concerns, but I am convinced it is best to start off with men alone; this establishes yours as a Man/Father Movement, as distinct from a Mom Follow-Along Movement.

The initial goal of these meetings is:

5) Identify your needs as Marathon Dads. Look at this question as you would any other business problem: brainstorm, then analyze. In the brainstorming phase, consider *all* of your needs as working fathers, regardless of whether the apparent resolution of these needs seems to lie within the workplace or outside of it. No editing now. No need should be considered too trivial ("I need more time first thing in the morning to get my head together before I dig into my work") or too grand ("I need to spend two solid afternoons a week with my teenage son if he's going to come through this rough period in one piece") to put on the table.

Analyze all of your needs for commonalities. Which needs or kinds of needs seem to come up most often? Child-care needs? Flexible-schedule needs? Stress-reduction needs? Again, take complete notes.

Such meetings can also become forums for discussing problems that you may have (and probably share) on the home front, say difficulty in communicating with your wife about task-distribution issues or tensions with your son when you supervise his homework. This gathering has the potential to evolve into a men's support group in the very best sense—without all the drumming and fire-in-the-belly stuff.

The next piece for this group to tackle is:

6) Brainstorm for new ways that your company can fulfill your needs as Marathon Dads. Some of these ways will be obvious to all of you by now—the institution of a flexible schedule, or paid paternity-leave options, or an on-site day-care center. But bone up on and discuss the ways the most advanced companies are meeting these needs. One method of doing this is to contact the Center for Work and Family (232 Baystate Road, Boston, MA 02215, 617-353-7225) and the Fatherhood Project at the Families and Work Institute in New York (330 Seventh Avenue, New York, NY 10001, 212-465-2044). Another way is to regularly consult relevant Web pages on the Internet (FatherNet can be reached at http://fsci. umn.edu/cyfc/cyfc.html).

But try not to limit these brainstorming sessions to known

practices. All you really know is that what worked for men
before does not work for you now, so any possible innovation
is a viable candidate. What can you collectively dream up that
would make your collective lives more efficient, more effective, and less stressful? Again, consider everything from the
most trivial-sounding ("I'd like to be able to arrive at work
fifteen minutes later so I can drive my kid to school") to the
most extravagant ("My life would be a whole lot easier if they
had a day-care and after-school center on the plant campus,
complete with homework tutors and computers").

7) Make your case with management. Decide among
you who is the best person to approach first with your proposals. Your immediate superior? Your union representative?
Your Family/Work officer? The CEO? Set a meeting with
that person.

Next, decide who of you is going to attend this meeting.
Just you (the de facto leader)? You and two or three other
men? (Generally, I find this option best—it shows support,
but is manageable.) You and two or three other men and
women? (A hard call, but I'd say save your women colleagues
for future meetings and negotiations so as not to dilute the
idea that these are men's issues.)

Be prepared for this meeting. That means a detailed memo/
agenda that lays out all the research you have done, the needs
you have identified, and your proposed solutions in the form
of new company policies. Have copies for everyone who will
be there.

Your main goal at this initial meeting is to *educate* management on your needs and *how the company stands to benefit
by meeting these needs.* This is not some phony trade-off, but
a way to genuinely increase productivity, creativity, morale,
and, ultimately, loyalty. Be very clear on that and why it is
true. These are not merely touchy-feely issues, nor are they
exclusively mom issues. Let your employers know that this is
an opportunity for them to be in the vanguard of a cultural

change that is going to happen whether or not they come on board now. Also let them know that you, as Marathon Dads, are ready to assume the leadership and responsibility for these changes, that they represent your priorities and total life needs, so you are no longer leaving all of the leadership and responsibility for these changes to working mothers.

Do not let this meeting end without setting up another meeting to discuss management's responses to your ideas. And keep following through with regular meetings until you are satisfied with the changes that are happening.

This is not easy, any of it, and especially not this final step. As in any real negotiation, you have to be prepared to back up your demands with alternative action—ultimately, that you are willing to look for employment elsewhere if your basic demands cannot be met. This is a major step for any man, especially a man with a family. But the bottom line is, if you truly believe in your priorities of being a first-rate worker and a first-rate father, and these priorities cannot be fulfilled unless your employer helps you fulfill them, then your choice is clear.

17

Marathon Dad–A Legacy
for the 21st Century

▼ ▼ ▼ ▼

The successful Marathon Dads whom I have come to know in these past few years all tell me how fortunate they feel to be living at this particular time in the History of Men. They say:

"I get to be there as my children grow up, something my father and his father never got to do."

And, *"There are so many more levels to my relationship with my wife—it's the best working partnership I've ever had."*

And, *"It took some doing to dig out my real priorities and then to figure out how to make them a reality, but it's all well worth it—I am a truly fulfilled man."*

These are men who will pass along a new legacy of what it means to be a fulfilled man to the coming generations. We are, indeed, Historical Heroes.

Let us conclude this journey by looking back at those seemingly insurmountable **Irreconcilable Differences** between being a **First-Rate Father** and a **First-Rate Professional** that faced us at the outset. But this time we can read them with a new consciousness. Indeed, I am confident that we can now call them:

Reconcilable Differences

1. **He puts Fatherhood on a par with—or ahead of— every other endeavor in his life/He puts Career on a par with—or ahead of—every other endeavor in his life.**

Our Heads: A man who constantly feels divided allegiances and dithers between them is a man who will always be beset by guilt and confusion. But *two* allegiances do not have to mean *divided* allegiances. If you know your own priorities and trust your judgment to pick them out as alternatives present themselves, you will not feel constantly torn between two masters. You simply know that your child comes first in certain situations and that your business comes first in others; you know that when, by your standards, your child *really* needs you and no one else, you will be there and nothing will stand in your way. The key to getting there is by embracing the fact that *you* are ultimately the only person in charge of setting your own priorities—not your wife, not your boss, and not your kids.

Our Practices: We think through and establish a checklist of priorities—maxims for choices that we can feel comfortable with and confident in. An easy example of a priority: *family medical emergencies always take precedence over any demand at work.* A tougher example: *a high fever rarely counts as a medical emergency.* Once we establish clear priorities, we will behave consistently.

We communicate our priorities loud and clear to everyone involved both at home and at work so that there are seldom any surprises on either front. Our children are secure in the knowledge that when they *really* need us, we will be there for them; our boss and fellow workers are secure in the knowledge that when they *really* need us, we will be there for them. Finally, we are always open to revising our priorities based on input from others at work and at home.

Our Politics: A major fallout of the above communication will be to set new collective standards of what are legitimate demands of family and work as compared to what are merely artifacts from outdated gender politics and power politics. We set an example that helps everyone sort out which policies contribute to productivity and which simply continue to contribute to make-work and arbitrary tests of loyalty. Our personal example says: *I can be loyal to my job without being a slave to it; and I can be loyal to my family without indulging its every desire.*

2. He never uses work obligations as an excuse for doing less than his share of work at home or for being less than a fully committed father/He never uses fatherhood obligations as an excuse for doing less than a first-rate job and he never does less than his share at work because of family obligations.

Our Heads: The common denominator here is excuse-making, a veritable industry for many of us. Our mothers were right about this one: if we are looking for an excuse for not doing something, we'll find one—and it will even sound pretty good. The reason we make excuses is because they work (in the short term) and because we can get away with them. For many men, excuses are a cultural habit on the home front: we heard our fathers make them all the time.

But making excuses turns out to be *extremely* counterproductive for Marathon Dads. Excuse-making is the psychological ally of a divided-loyalties mind-set; as long as we are busy making excuses for doing A rather than B, we never have to get around to *prioritizing A and B*. The end result is that we spend more time and energy making excuses than we would if we resolved our priorities and put an end to our need for excuses. We finally realize that if our task has become that of excusing ourselves from tasks, we have lost focus on what we really want to get done.

Our Practices: Because we have established and communicated our priorities, we find ourselves making fewer and fewer excuses at home and at work. We don't have to anymore, because everyone knows what to expect of us. As a result, we are far better focused and get more done in both places.

Our Politics: Giving up excuse-making represents a bigger cultural shift than most of us would imagine. In the old family culture when women did not go to work, men were pretty much expected to use their jobs as an excuse for not pitching in at home. That doesn't cut it now; still, it is taking a long time for family culture to adjust to that fact, and it is the responsibility of Marathon Dad to help that adjustment along.

On the other hand, some working mothers have allowed excuse-making to seep into the new workplace culture— excuses on the order of "I didn't do a good job because I was too busy being a good mommy." Permitting excuse-making at work is a cultural shift that ultimately is counterproductive for both working mothers and working fathers; the political responsibility of Marathon Dad here is to resist such a cultural shift.

3. He shares equally with his wife the workload of being a parent/He meets all professional expectations and deadlines.

Our Heads: We start by admitting to ourselves once and for all that times have changed, women are staying in the workforce, so we have to get past the old "I already gave at work" mind-set. But by the same token, we recognize that one reason we resist equally sharing the workload at home is because we confuse *equal tasks* with *identical tasks*; we confuse doing home tasks in a *characteristically male/fatherly way* with doing them in a *neutered parental way*, a way that may not come easily or naturally to us. (No, I am not setting up some macho excuse for getting out of work here, just introducing a critical distinction that runs throughout this book: namely, that *a daddy is not a mommy*.) Getting beyond these confusions requires resisting a load of guilt, some of it perpetuated by confused wives.

Similarly, as professionals who meet all on-the-job expectations and deadlines, we value our own personal style of doing our job; we realize that we do not have to conform to some anonymous model of a good worker as long as we get the job done. We are confident and secure enough to take advantage of changes in the workplace that have been brought about by working mothers (say flex time) without being cowed by male stereotypes (like, "Only a wimp would take flex time").

Our Practices: At home, we negotiate with our wives a way of doing our fair share of the second shift, and then we do our fair share without making excuses. *But we explicitly reserve the right to do our share in our own way, preserving our own fathering aptitudes and styles.* For example, we may declare that we will share diaper-changing duties, but we also declare that *we* decide when and how we will do it—mothers cannot insist on being the "experts" who make those decisions for us.

At work, we learn from pioneering working mothers which of the new family/work programs actually work and which do not. As long as we are able to continue doing a first-rate job while using these programs, we are not afraid to use them.

Our Politics: We participate in a major shift here—from the lingering pre-women-at-work division of labor (women own the second shift) to a division of home tasks determined by fairness. We begin negotiating our tasks with our wives by immediately acknowledging we want to reach parity; but we also insist that they respect our personal and characteristic gender differences in doing our share. We define ourselves in the workplace as someone committed to doing an A-one job *and* being an equal-share parent.

Both of these political positions involve revised definitions of being a man; at home, we define being a father as categorically different from being a mother; at work, we define being a male worker with parenting responsibilities as categorically *similar* to being a female worker with parenting responsibilities—and we do not apologize for that similarity.

4. He embraces every aspect of fathering, from Nurturer to Disciplinarian to Teacher to Drudge Worker/ He does whatever it takes to get his job done well, from taking on leadership to doing drab-but-necessary tasks.

Our Heads: We do not let stereotypes of fatherhood foisted on us by women, other men, our parents, and popular culture prevent us from taking on this role in all of its varieties and complexities. We acknowledge that being a father is *not* one thing.

When it comes to the ever-present problem of doing the drudge work of parenting, we find that reconciliation comes by applying a standard from our work lives to our home lives: At one time or another, most of us have done some drudge work in order to bring in needed income and most of us are proud of having done so; but at home, many of us have drawn the line at doing crap work (literally, as in changing a diaper) because we are *too proud* to do it, because we persist in calling it "women's work." A fond farewell to that stereotype.

We are now ready to acknowledge the fact that there is the same honor in doing drudge work at home as there is to doing it to earn money. Similarly, we are also ready to acknowledge that there is the same honor in being a "team player" at home as there is in being a "team player" at work.

Our Practices: We do the jobs we say we will do at both work and home.

Our Politics: Again, we are point men in the major cultural shift from fathers who do not do their fair share to fathers who do.

5. He is never afraid to stand up for the idea of Fatherhood that he believes in—both at work *and* with his

wife/He is never afraid to take a stand on a professional idea that he believes in.

Our Heads: The common denominators here are *confidence* and *independence of thought*. We need them both to resist the stereotypes of fatherhood and maleness that everyone and his mother (literally) seem to want to foist on us. As confident and independent Marathon Dads, we will not let anyone else define us or our roles, not a wife who insists on being the "expert" at home, not a male peer who insists that only wimps take paternity leave.

Our Practices: We go public with our personal convictions at both home and work. (Otherwise, we haven't really taken a stand anywhere but in our heads.) We absorb the consequences of our stands, including enduring some marital conflict and some peer disapproval.

Our Politics: Our convictions become maxims for cultural change, but this works only if they are backed up with a high level of performance and productivity. This, in fact, is the key to *every* political stand we take as Marathon Dad professionals: *we can be an agent of change toward a father-friendly work culture only if we continue to do uncompromised and outstanding professional work.*

6. He loves his children and is never afraid to show it/ He loves his job and is never afraid to show it.

Our Heads: Showing our kids our love for them is one thing, but showing our love for our kids *to our fellow workers* is quite another. Likewise, showing our enthusiasm for our job to our co-workers and bosses is one thing, but showing our enthusiasm for our job *to our families* is quite another. It takes supreme confidence to resist the shaming pressures of both a jealous boss and a jealous family. It takes a great deal of self-knowledge and a strong heart to finally stop telling those old, habitual lies: *"I hate my job because it takes me away from* you," and *"My family is a real drag because it keeps me from doing the work I really love to do."*

Just as giving up excuse-making allows us to have clearer heads and more tranquil, guilt-free hearts, giving up those lies liberates us too. We dare to love our families deeply without having to pretend that we don't love our professional lives as well. We dare to define our loyalty to our job on our own terms: "I do a damn good job and love my work, but that does not mean I have to sacrifice the rest of my life to prove it to my boss and co-workers." We get beyond the idea that we are always in a contest for what or whom we love the most. We are secure in what we *do* feel, and we really do not care what anybody else thinks we *should* feel.

Our Practices: We display our love proudly, but we do not give in to pressures for *exclusive* loyalty at either home or work. If our child says, in effect, "You can't love both your job and me. Show me you love me more!" tell him that it's not a contest, that you consider yourself very fortunate to have a life that has room for both a stimulating job and a happy, loving family life. If our boss says, in effect, "Show me your loyalty to your job by being here whenever I need you. When you sacrifice your family time, you show your loyalty to your job and there's no substitute for that," tell him that he can tell how dedicated you are to your job only by how well you do it—end of story.

Our Politics: Our mission at work is to lead our co-workers and bosses to the point where they can accept the idea that loyalty and dedication to our job is best judged by our performance at that job. Our mission at home is to lead our wives and children to the point where they can accept the idea that we can love them unconditionally while still loving our professional lives. And letting them know that loving us means loving us in our totality, both parent and worker.

7. He never apologizes to his employer or colleagues for his loyalty to his family/ He never apologizes to his family for his loyalty to his job.

Our Heads: Working fathers fall all too easily into the habit of automatic apology-making: "I'm sorry, son, I really wish I could come to the ball game this afternoon, but I've got an important meeting"; and "I'm sorry, George, I really wish I could come to that meeting this afternoon, but I promised my son I'd go to the ball game with him." Sure, it is virtuous to admit our mistakes when we make them, but when offering an apology becomes our mind-set and modus operandi at work and at home, we weaken our own confidence, make ourselves into ditherers, and encourage everyone around us to lose confidence in us. The apologies start to control us. Apology-making becomes the pathetic twin of excuse-making, another way to avoid setting priorities and feeling comfortable with them. Our task here is clear: stop it—put an end to our automatic apology-making mechanism where it begins, in our heads.

Our Practices: The way we put an end to our apology-making mind-set is the same way we finished off our excuse-making mind-set: by setting clear priorities and broadcasting them. When everybody knows what to expect, no apologies are necessary.

Our Politics: Apology-making can become a veritable culture, especially at home, where our children may start to think of us as *Dad, the Apology Maker*. This is a culture of weakness and guilt for *everyone* involved. (The kids experience guilt for feeling angry at us for disappointing them—"How can I be angry? Dad *did* apologize for missing his fifteenth ball game in a row.") Everybody wins when we stop with the apologies.

8. He is mindful of planning his family duties/He recognizes the cardinal importance of time management as a professional.

Our Heads: A persistent myth at home is that family time is fundamentally different from work time: it needs to be loose and spontaneous, so it would be "unnatural" to try to manage it. We fear treating our family like another client; we are uncomfortable with the "coldness" implicit in scheduling family time and family duties. This, of course, turns out to be a convenient alibi for not putting in enough time at home, spontaneous or otherwise; the resistance to thinking about family time in an organized way defeats it from happening at all. Consider the analogy to marital sex by appointment/schedule: we tend to resist this system because it is unromantic, unspontaneous; reduces sex to another thing to cross off our list. However, the statistical fact is that most working couples who don't schedule sex rarely find time to do it. So the question remains: is spending *unspontaneous* time with our family better than hardly ever spending time with them at all? The answer is, of course, that we have to start managing our time for/at home as rigorously as we manage it at work.

A quite different myth prevents us from managing our time at work in a way that allows us to both get our jobs done and be hands-on fathers: we persist in believing that the *more* time we spend on the job, the better it is (and the better *we* are.) But the reality is that in a product-oriented workplace, *the quality of what gets done* is ultimately more important than simply how many hours a worker put in that week. Just as we are discovering that the concept of *Quality Time* does not cut it at home, we are discovering that the concept of *Quality Time* can be very meaningfully applied at work.

Another basic mind-set that keeps us from better parceling out our time between home and work is the one that says: *"My time at work is out of my control—I've got bosses, co-workers, and meetings determining my schedule—but at home, time is more flexible, so my wife and family can accommodate my schedule."* Nice try, but this one is at least partially wrong on both counts: first, we actually do have more control of our time at work than most of us believe (that is, if we decide to take control of it); and second, home time is getting less flexible by the minute in a house with both parents working.

Our Practices: We schedule our time at home with the same foresight, consideration, care, and communication with which we schedule our work time. This includes taking into account the time demands of all the members of the family. One key concept here is distinguishing between managing home time *efficiently* and managing it *effectively*—that is, with the focus on what will be accomplished with this particular allotted time. For example, being with your toddler at 3 P.M. may be a lot more *effective* than being with her from eight to ten at night. Again, priority-setting informs effective home-time scheduling; among other things, it keeps us from getting carried away by every "crisis" and "emergency."

Our Politics: We make our work schedules known at home and our home schedules known at work. And we prove that these schedules work by *doing both jobs effectively*. We know we are in a position to take the lead in using family-time opportunities at work or to lobby for them if they are not in place yet. In short, we take a strong position against the "Wimp Factor."

9. He acknowledges his place in the Historical Legacy of Fatherhood/He acknowledges his place in the Historical Legacy of a Professional Worker.

Our Heads: Here we get into a tricky but critical balancing act. The tradition of fatherhood clearly needs to change in the new economy, yet we still must hold on to what is good in that tradition. We start by taking a clear-eyed look at traditional fatherhood and the myths that surround it. For example, were the '50s fathers really as heartless, superficial, and uninvolved as the revisionists would have us believe? Some people out there (mostly women) argue that we have to junk everything about fatherhood we ever learned, especially from our own dads. Really? If we do that, all we'll have left as a role model is Mom. On the other hand, we recognize that motherhood has had to change too, that it has had to reinvent itself while hanging on to motherhood traditions. We need to look at the places where traditional roles have to change, but we should be careful not to throw out the baby with the bathwater. Similarly, the traditions of the work culture need to change, but we must be mindful of which of those traditions we should hang on to—for example, basic job loyalty, teamwork, responsibility, etc.

Our Practices: Our job here can be a lonely one. We stand firm against those who want us to junk every aspect of traditional fatherhood, but we also stand firm against those people (mostly men) who call our willingness to reinvent fatherhood a betrayal. We contend with revisionist views without sounding like (or becoming) pigs who do not want to change, and we demonstrate to both co-workers and family members that some changes can work to everyone's advantage.

Our Politics: We become an example of a father and a professional who embraces traditional values while seeking new ways to effect them.

10. He champions good fatherhood with his fellow fathers/He champions Professionalism with his fellow workers.

Our Heads, Our Practices, and Our Politics: Here is where the personal becomes the political. We are Marathon Dads and proud of it. We are prepared, at work and at home, for both working fathers and working mothers to lead the way.

Take the Lead!